2

MARC CHAGALL

Russian

1889-

DOUBLE PORTRAIT WITH A GLASS OF WINE

Musée National d'Art Moderne, Paris

Marc Chagall was born in Vitebsk, Russia. He was one of a large and poor family; nevertheless, his parents recognized his talent and he received his first art lessons in his native village before going to St. Petersburg to study with Leon Bakst, the theatrical designer. In St. Petersburg, Chagall had his first contact with European and French contemporary art and was encouraged in his own ideas. He went to Paris in 1910 and was soon a member of the large group of foreign artists living in Montmartre. Chagall's first large exhibition was held in Berlin in 1914. He spent the war years in Russia and in 1917 was appointed by the Revolutionary government to an important post. However, Chagall disagreed with other Russian artists, resigned his post, and, after a short period in Moscow, designing murals and sets for the Jewish Theatre there, he returned to Paris in 1922. His reputation was firmly established by that time and he received commissions to illustrate several books, the most important being the Bible, for which he travelled to the Holy Land to visit the sites he drew. Chagall spent the years of the Nazi occupation of France in the United States, having been invited by the Museum of Modern Art. He returned to France late in the 1940's and settled in Vence; he now divides his time between that place and Paris, painting, designing stained-glass windows, and giving away his great public works, such as those for the United Nations, the Jerusalem Synagogue, the Paris Opera, and the new home of the New York Metropolitan Opera at Lincoln Center. Chagall is a Surrealist in a poetic and happy manner, painting, in vivid colors and with great imagination, a marvelous world of fantasy and delight.

3

PABLO PICASSO
Spanish
1881-

THE LOVERS

National Gallery of Art, Washington, D.C.
Chester Dale Collection

Pablo Ruiz Picasso was born in Malaga, Spain. The son of an art teacher, he had a sound, early academic training. When he was fourteen, the family moved to Barcelona and Picasso had his first exhibition there in 1897. He made his first trip to Paris in 1900, staying for a few months and beginning to paint in an Impressionistic manner. The following year he launched a new magazine in Barcelona, *Arte Joven* (Young Art), and made a second trip to Paris, and then a third, the following year. He settled in Paris in 1904, painting three pictures a day. His output has always been prodigious, as drawing and painting are as natural as breathing to him. Picasso has remained in France, except for a summer trip to Spain in 1909, for over sixty years. From 1904 until 1906 he painted his Blue and Rose Period works. Then followed a brief period of a few months during which his works showed the influence of African sculpture. This culminated in *Les Demoiselles D'Avignon,* a great work in which hints of Cubism are already present. From 1907 until 1915, he and Braque were the leaders of the Cubist school, based on a complete application of the principles of Cézanne. This movement led to a major revolution in European art. At the close of World War I, Braque and Picasso abandoned pure Cubism to go their separate ways. Picasso began to work in a Classical and sculpturesque manner, but also made Surrealist theater and ballet sets and costumes. Beginning in the year 1923, Picasso worked in a variety of styles combining his previous manners and adding new ones. His double portraits, a form of Expressionism particularly his own, first appeared in 1938. Since that time he has worked in every medium and manner, passing from one to the other with ease, according to the demands of the particular piece of work he is doing, whether it be an easel painting, a fresco, illustrations for books, a large sculpture, or small ceramics.

The Lovers is purely romantic in color, pose, attitudes of the subjects, and expressions. The woman is almost coy, the man gentle and tender. One thinks inevitably of Romeo and Juliet when looking at this work, for the coloring, although applied in light transparencies, is brilliant—turquoise blue, red, green, yellow, grey-violet, and grey. The woman's headpiece and veil are medieval or Renaissance in feeling, and her garments are classical draperies, while the lover is wearing what we may imagine, if we so choose, to be doublet and hose. Picasso's strong drawing removes sentimentality and focuses on the full strength of love.

4

SALVADOR DALI

Spanish

1904-

THE SACRAMENT OF THE LAST SUPPER

National Gallery of Art, Washington, D.C.
Chester Dale Collection

Salvador Dali was born in Figueras, Spain. His father was a notary from Cadaques on the Costa Brava. The Dali family spent their summers in Cadaques and its landscape is familiar to us, as it appears over and over in Dali's paintings. Dali began his career as an *enfant terrible* in the schools of Figueras and then went to the School of Fine Arts in Madrid. He learned the fundamentals of drawing easily and well, but he was really interested in studying Freud and art magazines that specialized in Cubism, Futurism, and metaphysical art. In his early work he tried to combine the Cubism of Chirico and Juan Gris with the techniques of the old masters. He went to Paris in about 1928 and attached himself to the French Surrealists with passionate conviction. In 1928 he married Gala Eluard, who appears in his paintings almost as frequently as does Cadaques. When Dali became absorbed by Italian Renaissance painting, the French Surrealists disowned him as much too academic and backward in technique. He left France for New York, where his popular success

has been due as much to his art as to his showmanship, which ranges from his book, published in 1942, *The Secret Life of Salvador Dali,* a sort of Freudian exhibitionism, to fancy costumes and poses and outlandish statements. Dali now divides his time between New York and Cadaques with flashing trips to other places where his works are shown.

Dali is a superb draughtsman and Surrealist. In *The Sacrament of the Last Supper* his draughtsmanship and balanced composition combine to make a classical work with limited Surrealistic additions. The Sea of Galilee is the familiar coastline of Cadaques and above the head of Christ and His disciples is a headless male figure with outstretched arms, a symbol either of Christ on the Cross or of God the Father, whose face we are powerless to see. The work is painted in muted tones of pale grey and paler gold; the atmosphere is misty as if the scene were taking place in the pale light of dawn lighted by an invisible moon.

5

TSUGOUHARU FOUJITA

Japanese

1886-

CAFE

Musée National d'Art Moderne, Paris

Tsugouharu Foujita was born in Japan. He was a pupil of the Imperial School of Fine Arts in Tokyo and by 1910 had received several medals and prizes. The Emperor purchased one of his paintings in 1910, and on a trip to Korea in 1911 he was asked to paint the sovereign of that country. Foujita seemed destined for a career in the Orient until he travelled to London in 1912 and went to live in Paris in 1913. He discovered European contemporary art much as the nineteenth-century French had discovered Japanese prints. Foujita had his first exhibition in Paris in 1917. By 1924 he was one of the most important exhibitors at the Salon d'Automne in Paris and in the same year was elected a member of the Tokyo Academy of Fine Arts, for he was the first Japanese artist to free that country's art of its legendary and classic image. Foujita was then selected to decorate the Japanese House at the Cité Universitaire in Paris. He travelled to England, Belgium, Holland, Switzerland, Italy, Germany, and the United States, where he had a studio until 1939. He returned to Paris at the outbreak of World War II and remained there until 1941, when he returned to Tokyo, staying reluctantly until 1950 when he went back to live in Paris. Foujita, a Chevalier of the Legion of Honor and of the Order of Leopold I of Belgium, still lives in Paris, where he paints and occupies himself with charitable functions as president of the Association of Japanese Artists.

Café is a rendering of a typical Parisian scene done in Foujita's delicate and decorative linear style and in his palette of sensitive pale grays, reddish-browns, and blacks. The mood is quiet and poetic, made more so by the Japanese traditional pattern subtly imposed on Western technique.

6

JOAN MIRO
Spanish
1893-

COMPOSITION 1963
Narodni Galerie, Prague

Joan Miró was born in Montroig in the province of Catalonia, Spain. He began the study of art at the Barcelona School of Fine Arts when he was fourteen. After a short while he enrolled at the Gali Academy in the same city. When he was eighteen, he decided that academic instruction was not giving him anything very useful and he decided to work alone. Upon his first visit to Paris in 1919 he came under the influence of Braque and Picasso and for a time painted in the Cubist manner. By 1925, however, he had become a member of the Surrealist group, exhibited with them in their first show, and his work took on the style and character now associated with his name. At about this time he worked with Max Ernst on the sets and costumes of *Roméo et Juliette,* a Diaghilev Ballet Russe production. His famous *Harlequin's Carnival,* now in the Albright-Knox Art Gallery in Buffalo, was painted at this time also. In 1928 Miró traveled to Holland and was exhibited for the first time in New York. He then began a production of *collages,* shown in Paris in 1930, and in 1937 painted a large mural for the Paris Exhibition. Miró left France in 1940 and went to the island of Majorca, where he continued to paint, began to make lithographs, and, with Artigas, did ceramic work. He returned to Paris in 1944 and now divides his time between that city and Barcelona. He paints, sculpts in wood (later painted) or stone, designs tapestries and rugs, and makes ceramics.

7

MAURICE de VLAMINCK

French

1876-1958

LES CHAUMIERES

Musée National d'Art Moderne, Paris

Maurice de Vlaminck was born in the heart of Paris, near Les Halles. His parents were both musicians of talent, although neither of them was well-known. Vlaminck (the name indicates his Flemish origin) began to draw while in elementary school and neglected his studies for his sketches. However, as he grew up he showed talent as a violinist and as a champion bicycle rider, so that he did not decide to become a painter until 1900, when he met Derain. The sight of van Gogh's paintings further stimulated Vlaminck and he began to paint, as a Fauve, without any academic studies. Vlaminck was a giant of a man with tremendous energy and, as a young man, he painted furiously in a brilliant orange, red, and blue palette, wrote novels and articles between paintings, and often went off on his bicycle at breakneck speed. As an older man he was a demon at the wheel of fast automobiles, often terrifying his daughters and his wife as he sped around curves. After 1915 Vlaminck's palette became more somber and more romantic, and his style grew in solidity, although it was always turbulent. Vlaminck remained resolutely apart from all trends of contemporary art that followed Fauvism, strange for one who had himself been so revolutionary. In 1935 he retired to a large farm, La Tourillière, near Beauce, continued to paint, and occupied himself with agriculture, as had his Flemish ancestors.

The country in *Les Chaumières* is that of Vlaminck's ancestors, a country that stretches out flat for miles. A *chaumière* is a thatched cottage and one sees many of them in this area, with their overhanging roofs over whitewashed walls. A feeling of solid security and endurance emerges from this painting, as it does from the landscape, despite the stormy, windy atmosphere under a sky filled with dark, almost black, storm clouds. The houses hug the land; the storm will pass; and life will continue on its path just as the straight line of the road.

8

MAURICE UTRILLO
French
1883-1955
A STREET IN THE SUBURBS
Narodni Galerie, Prague

Maurice Utrillo was born in Paris, the illegitimate child of Suzanne Valadon and an amateur painter and chronic alcoholic named Boissy. The name Utrillo was given to the boy when he was eight years old by a Spanish art critic of that name. Maurice was an unhappy and neurotic child. The family lived in the country and, since he went to school in Paris, he formed the habit, in his early teens, of stopping off for a glass of wine before taking the train home each night. He did badly in school and had to be withdrawn to go to work as a bank clerk. By that time, the wine had become absinthe and Utrillo promptly lost his job. At the age of eighteen he had to be confined to an asylum for acute alcoholism. It was while he was shut away, the first of many such incarcerations, that he took up painting as a form of occupational therapy. It soon became as necessary for him to paint as to drink. He would drink all night and paint all day, and, if he had to be locked up, he painted from memory or from picture postcards. By 1920 he was famous all over the world, and by 1929 he had received the Legion of Honor. It was not until he was in his late fifties that he gave up drinking entirely, when he married a widow who watched over him carefully. He died, a respectable citizen, in a house that the couple purchased in one of the Parisian suburbs that Utrillo so loved to paint.

Utrillo is known as the painter of Montmartre and suburban streets. He also painted some cathedrals and country scenes, but these bulk very small in the large number of paintings he created. Entirely self-taught, he had an unerring painter's eye for color and perspective, with the taste to eliminate unnecessary details. Even in his gayest, later works there is a hint of melancholy and loneliness.

9

ALBERT MARQUET

French

1875-1947

ETE, LA PLAGE DES SABLES D'OLONNE

Musée National d'Art Moderne, Paris

Albert Marquet, who was born in Bordeaux, arrived in Paris, very young and very poor, to study at the School of Decorative Arts under Gustave Moreau. Matisse was also studying there at the time and, in order to earn money for the start of two promising careers, the two artists decorated the Paris Exposition halls in 1900 in Moreau's "art nouveau" style. Associated with Matisse in the 1903 Salons, Marquet was considered a Fauve, although he was in reality merely in revolt against Impressionism. For him, color was never an end or a means in itself. Once his career was safely launched, Marquet spent the rest of his life alternately at his studio on the Quai St. Michel in Paris painting the Seine and its bridges and in various seaports all over Europe and North Africa. He traveled constantly and whenever the spirit moved him, staying with painter friends until he was bored and then leaving as unexpectedly as he had arrived. Extremely independent and very shy, Marquet lived simply and quietly, painting as he liked, with no regard for public taste, and refusing all public honors. Marquet communicated with the world through his paintings and that was enough for him.

Eté, la Plage des Sables d'Olonne presents a crowded beach late in the day. Under a violet and blue sky the yellows and reds of the beach tents take on a purplish tint. Long shadows and mist on the sea add to the feeling of approaching night. Without sentimentality, Marquet reminds us that beach and water will soon be empty and deserted, and that the quiet of nature will be restored.

10

GEORGES ROUAULT

French

1871-1958

THE APPRENTICE

Musée National d'Art Moderne, Paris

Georges Rouault was born in Paris during the revolt of the Commune. His father, a cabinetmaker and an anti-Catholic, sent him to a Protestant school, from whose austerity Rouault escaped to the warmer atmosphere of the studio of a restorer of Medieval stained-glass windows. Rouault was an apprentice here at fourteen and this early work had a profound effect upon his career. He worked by day and studied at the School of Decorative Arts at night until 1891, when he became a pupil of Gustave Moreau at the Beaux-Arts. In 1895 Rouault embraced Catholicism. For some years after that his life and work were influenced by his friendship with Léon Bloy, a writer of spiritual but bitterly ironic tendencies, and with Joris K. Huysmans, the lavishly sensual author. Rouault's subjects embraced both the religious and the temporal, and in the latter area his warm humanity led him to portray the poor and miserable. He began his work as an engraver in 1917, illustrating many books and reaching his greatest heights in *Miserere and War,* published in 1947. It was in 1947, also, that Rouault regained from the heirs of his dealer, Vollard, a great many of his earlier paintings. He destroyed 315 that he considered imperfect, and devoted the rest of his life to working on others in an effort to achieve the standard of perfection he had set himself.

Rouault's sympathy for humanity and for the working classes makes of *The Apprentice* a figure not of the present but of some mythical past. With an economy of brushwork, he makes us feel pity and the misery of the human condition.

11

RAOUL DUFY

French

1877-1953

RIDERS IN THE FOREST

Musée National d'Art Moderne, Paris

Raoul Dufy was born in Le Havre. He began to work as an errand boy for a coffee importer when he was fourteen, and was soon working by day and studying art at night in the city's Municipal School of Art. He received a small scholarship in 1900 and went to Paris, where he studied with Bonnat and encountered Matisse and other young painters of the Fauve group. Dufy painted in the colors of the Fauves, but in a distinctly personal manner with light, curving strokes that fly across paper or canvas with lightning speed. Dufy's first acceptance by the official Salon occurred in 1910. During the following ten years he worked as a museum assistant, illustrated books, and designed silk fabrics to make a living. He travelled to the south of France, to Sicily, and to Morocco in 1920, seeking inspiration and material. By 1925 his reputation was solidly established and he was commissioned to paint murals for many French public buildings. He began to suffer from multiple arthritis in 1937 and moved to southwestern France for his health. Nevertheless, the disease progressed to the point where he could no longer paint, and in 1947 he came to the United States for cortisone treatment in Boston. After the treatment and a trip to Arizona, Dufy, though not cured, was well enough to return to France and to continue his own unique style of painting until his death a few years later.

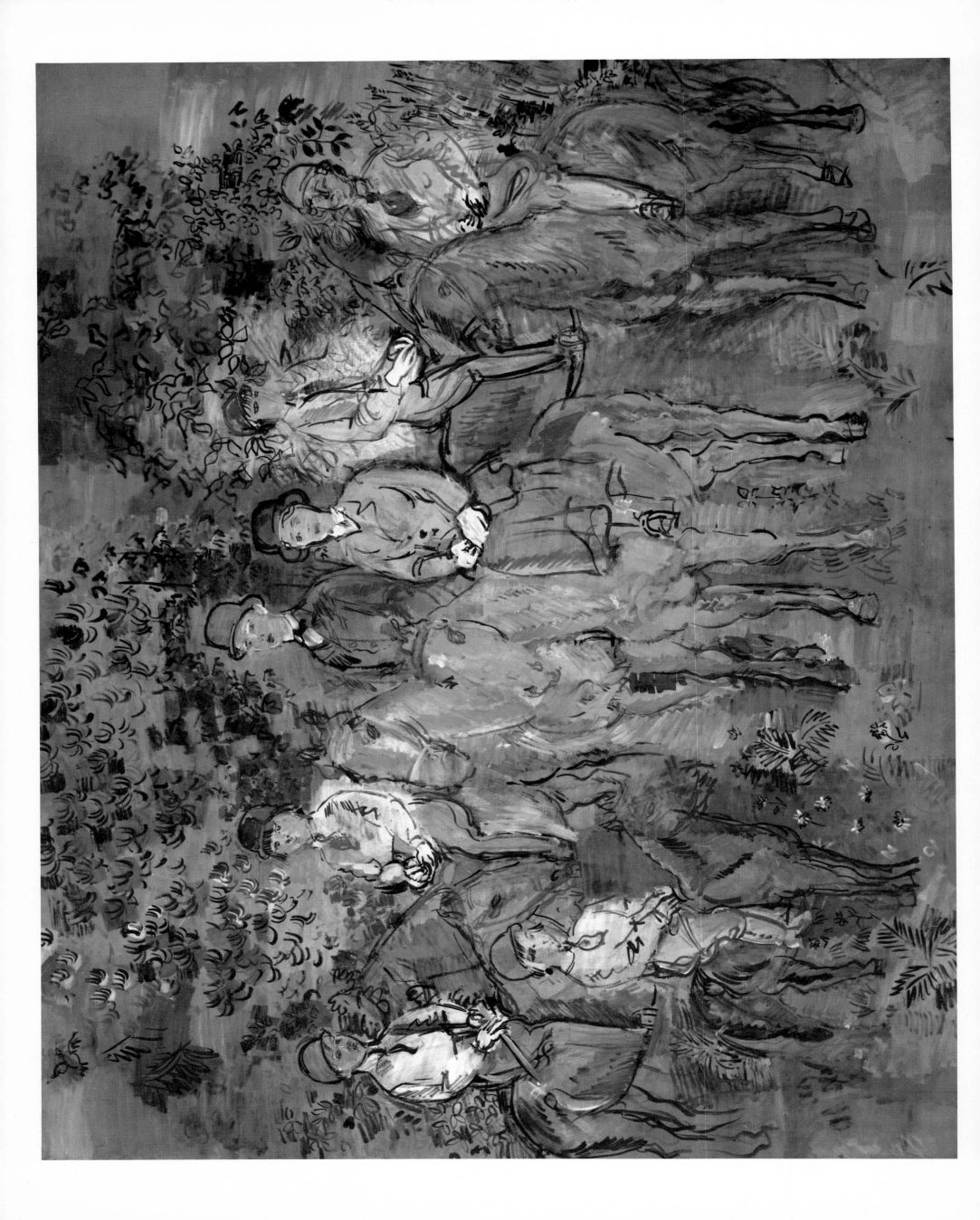

12

AMEDEO MODIGLIANI
Italian
1884-1920

GYPSY WOMAN WITH BABY

National Gallery of Art, Washington, D.C.
Chester Dale Collection

Amedeo Modigliani was born in the Livorno ghetto. His father, a ruined banker, died young, and his mother, a descendant of the Dutch philosopher, Spinoza, encouraged her delicate son in his aptitude for art, sending him to study in Florence and Venice and to visit museums throughout Italy. When Modigliani arrived in Paris in 1907, he had a small inheritance from a rich uncle, but he was already seriously ill with tuberculosis. Handsome, talented, sensitive, and extremely proud of his Jewish heritage, Modigliani became one of the most notorious characters in Montmartre and was soon penniless and often homeless. He frequently slept and worked in the studios of artist friends who liked him and recognized his great talent as both a painter and a sculptor. He moved to Montparnasse in 1913 and kept body and soul together by selling drawings in cafés for infinitesimal sums. He was sheltered for a time by an English poetess and then by a kindly art dealer named Zborowski. Finally, in 1917, he married Jeanne Hébuterne

and the couple set up housekeeping in a miserable garret. It was too late for this more normal life to conquer the ravages of consumption. Modigliani died in a Paris hospital on a January day in 1920. His desperate widow threw herself from the roof of her parents' apartment house on the day of his funeral, leaving their daughter to be reared by her maternal grandparents. Two years later Modigliani was discovered by Dr. Albert C. Barnes, the great art collector of Pennsylvania. Today his paintings and his sculpture, even unfinished, command high prices at art auctions.

Modigliani painted portraits and nudes in a distinctively stylized and mannered, almost Baroque fashion. His name immediately evokes sinuous, elegant line; dark backgrounds, golden or olive; Italianate skin tones; sloping shoulders; long, slender necks; faintly melancholy, dreaming, or empty eyes in oval faces. Within this frame, the artist's talent provided many variations.

13

EDWARD HOPPER

American

1882-

SEVEN A. M.

Collection of the Whitney Museum of American Art, New York

Edward Hopper was born in Nyack, New York. He studied art at the Chase School in New York under Chase, Miller, and Henri from 1900 to 1905 and became a follower of the Ashcan School, painting in a fairly dark and somber palette. He spent the years 1906 and 1907 in Paris. When he returned to the United States, his palette was considerably lighter and brighter than it had been. Hopper exhibited with the Independents in 1910 and again at the Armory Show in 1913. He sold his first painting, an oil, at the Armory show, but did not sell another until 1923, when he had a successful watercolor show. Between 1915 and 1923 Hopper worked as an etcher and a commercial artist, since he could not make a living from his paintings. When, after the 1923 show, he was able to give up commercial art and devote himself to painting in oils, he displayed a completely finished and highly personal style from which he has never deviated. Hopper's recognition came late, but it has included honorary university degrees and the Gold Medal of the National Institute of Arts and Letters.

This painting, *Seven A.M., 1948,* is a fine example of Hopper's realistic, starkly painted, lonely American scenes with a romantic overtone. The drugstore, with its drearily arranged and almost empty windows and its clock ticking away the empty hours, stands on the edge of a town where the sidewalk ends. In sharp contrast to the clearly lit and clean lines of the white shingled house and wooden store front, the dark green trees of the woods beyond convey a strange, frightening sensation. Loneliness, we feel, is only comparative, for who would leave even that barren shop for the mysterious things that lurk in the open country?

14

FRANZ MARC

German

1880-1916

BLUE HORSES

Collection Walker Art Center, Minneapolis

Franz Marc was born in Munich, Bavaria. His father, an artist, encouraged him to study art, but Marc studied theology and philosophy before entering the Munich Art Academy in 1900. Marc was a moody and often depressed young man and had difficulty in finding a way to express himself in paint. Upon his first trip to Paris in 1903, he had his first contacts with the Impressionists and was particularly impressed with the work of Henri Rousseau. In the following year, contact with the avant-garde *Jugendstil* group in Munich helped him to clarify his ideas. When he made a second trip to Paris in 1907, he saw the work of van Gogh. In 1910 he met Macke and Kandinsky and became a member of the *Blaue Reiter,* worked on the first almanac, and participated in the first *Blaue Reiter* exhibition in Germany. A meeting with Delaunay in 1912 finally set Marc on the road to his own form of expression and he began his paintings of animals, a subject he chose in order to free himself of subjectivity and sentimentality. Within a year he could paint landscapes and was well on the way toward abstraction. Unfortunately, Marc's career ended abruptly on the battlefield of Verdun in 1916. Of the last two years of his life, we have his notebook filled with drawings of a world of horror. What could we have learned from this man who wanted only to understand and be understood?

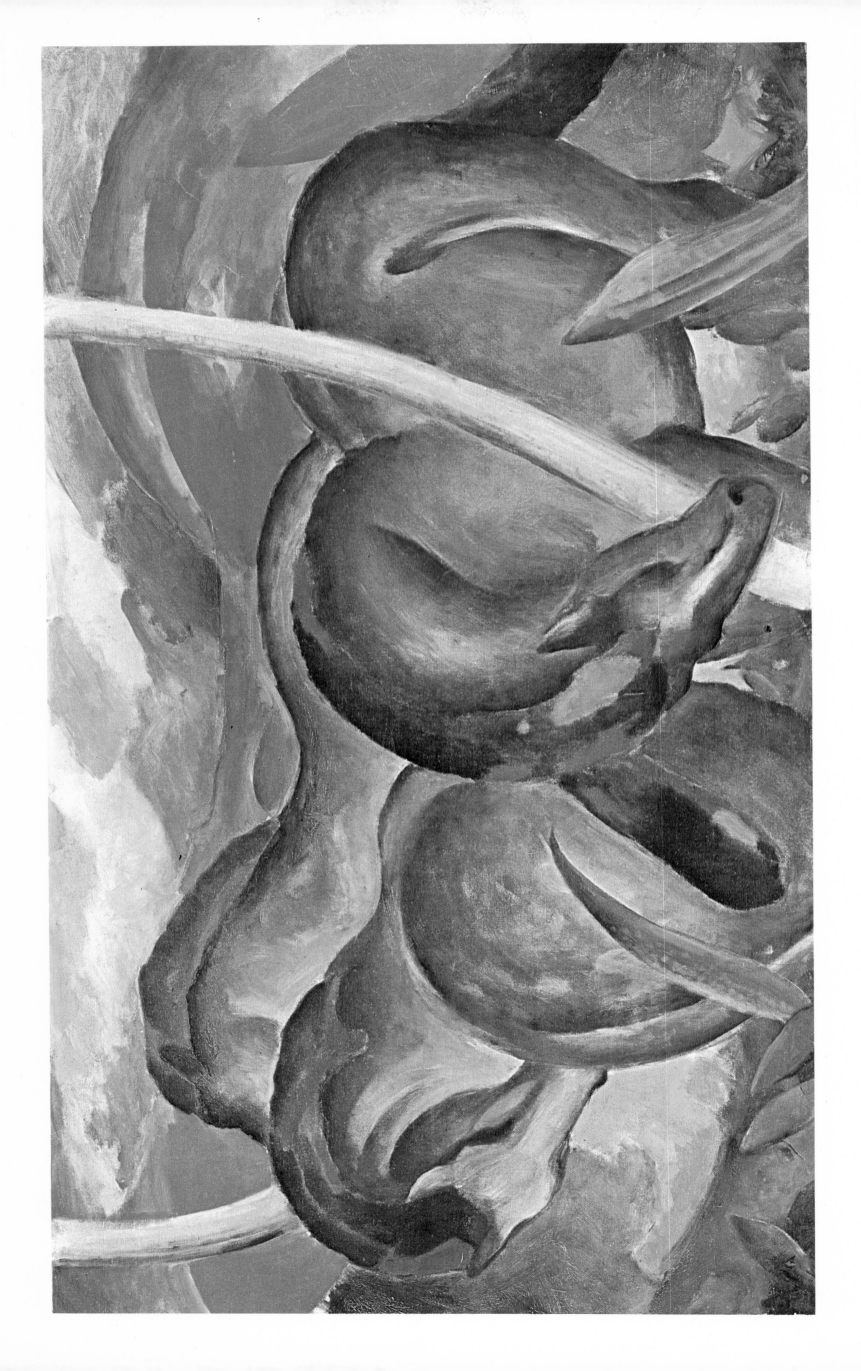

15

GEORGE BELLOWS
American
1882-1925

DEMPSEY AND FIRPO
Collection of the Whitney Museum of American Art, New York

George Bellows was born in Columbus, Ohio. He attended school in Columbus and then went to Ohio State University. He was probably the first artist who ever gave up a possible career as a major league baseball player in order to paint. He went to New York in 1904 and studied with Robert Henri and H. G. Maratta, before opening his own studio in 1906. A giant of a man with prodigious energy, Bellows turned out literally a flood of paintings from that time until his death. In 1908 he won the National Academy's first prize for landscape painting with the first landscape he painted. He was elected an associate of the National Academy a year later. Bellows was twenty-seven at the time and was one of the youngest men elected to the Academy in its history. Bellows became an instructor at the Art Students League in 1910, and later taught at the Ferrer School and the Art Institute of Chicago. His earliest work was of the Ash-

can School genre, but his interest soon shifted to scenes of muscular strength, landscapes, and portraits. Bellows began to work as a lithographer in 1916 and produced a great many fine prints. His career came to an abrupt and untimely end in 1925, when he died of an attack of acute appendicitis to whose first symptoms he had paid no attention.

Dempsey and Firpo is one of many fight paintings that Bellows produced—evidence of his lifelong interest in athletes and especially boxers. The work has a crashing vitality and is as startling to the viewer as the hurtling body projected out of the ring is to the startled spectators, who jump backward, stare with open mouths, and behave, generally, as people do at fights when they are shocked by an extraordinary blow. The palette is limited in color, the light is focused on the ring, and the composition is packed with dynamic force.

16

PAUL KLEE

Swiss

1879-1940

SENECIO

Kunstmuseum Basel
©Cosmopress and Spadem 1966 by French Reproduction Rights, Inc.
Photograph: Colorphoto Hinz, Basel

Paul Klee was born near Berne, Switzerland. His Swiss mother was an amateur painter and his Bavarian father was a professor of music. As a child, Klee showed both musical and artistic talent, but finally decided to become an artist and went to Munich to study at the Fine Arts Academy. Klee's first exhibition was held in Berne in 1910. It showed the influence of Cézanne, Matisse, and van Gogh. In 1912, Klee exhibited with the *Blaue Reiter*. By the following year he had begun to state, in a series of essays that appeared in Zurich, his own personal, spiritual approach to art. It must be noted that Klee's earlier work was almost entirely in black and white, pencil or ink, varied occasionally by watercolor. However, in 1914 he made a trip to Tunisia with Macke and the possibilities of working in color became apparent to him. All of his oils, therefore, were painted between 1914 and 1940. Klee was invited to teach at the Bauhaus in Weimar in 1920 and continued with that school until 1931. He was made Professor of Fine Arts in Düsseldorf in 1931.

The Nazis included nine of Klee's works in the "degenerate" art exhibition of 1933, invaded his studio, and suspended him from his post. Klee was able, luckily, to take his paintings, drawings, and writings with him when he sought refuge in Berne, where he continued to work until his death in 1940.

Klee uses the simplest geometrical forms for *Senecio (Head of a Man)* and arranges them on what seem to be childlike principles. The head, however, that seems at first to be wooden and without expression, comes to life as we look at it; the red eyes breathe fire; one of them reflects another image; the arched eyebrow asks a question. Suddenly the face turns into that of a cat. As suddenly, it is everyman's face, difficult to comprehend and secretive—a head full of ideas for evil or for good. The evil is in the eyes; and the good is in the color —soft pinks and yellows. The mystery is in the mouth—tiny, buttoned-up in contrast to the wide-open eyes. Klee is another name for provocative.

17

MAURICE PRENDERGAST

American

1859-1924

CENTRAL PARK, 1901

Collection of the Whitney Museum of American Art, New York

Maurice Prendergast was born in St. John's, Newfoundland. His family moved to Boston when he and his brother, Charles, were boys. Maurice began his career in Boston as an apprentice to a maker of showcards, working first as a washer of brushes and working up to lettering cards. He spent his weekends wandering about Boston and painting. By 1886 he had saved enough money, one thousand dollars, to go abroad. He and his brother worked their way over on a cattle boat. Maurice studied painting in Paris, first at the Académie Julian and then at the Académie Colarossi. When the brothers returned to the United States, they settled in Winchester, Massachusetts, where Charles became a frame-carver, assisted by Maurice who, however, continued to paint. Maurice went abroad again in 1898, helped by his patroness, Mrs. Montgomery Sears, and painted in Venice and St.-Malo. His last trip abroad was to Italy in 1912. After that, he settled in New York, again with his brother. Prendergast worked in watercolor until he was too old to paint outdoors and then turned to oils. The general public remained indifferent to his work until 1923, when he received a 2,000-dollar prize at the Corcoran Biennial Exhibition.

Prendergast was a most original, delightful, and individualistic painter. He worked in his own style which stems from Impressionism and moves toward Divisionism, a series of small squares of pure, pale color that interlock like stitches in a tapestry to form a pattern as one moves away from the painting. In *Central Park, 1901* the pattern moves outward from a shallow perspective that is, however, less important to the composition than the repeated horizontals. In pale greens and yellows, brightened by the red of carriage wheels, a scene emerges that is perfectly delightful in its delicate sunny sedateness and gentle movement.

18

WILLIAM JAMES GLACKENS

American

1870-1938

CENTRAL PARK IN WINTER

The Metropolitan Museum of Art, New York
George A. Hearn Fund, 1921

William James Glackens was born in Philadelphia. He began his career as an illustrator for the *Philadelphia Press* and other newspapers, studying at the Pennsylvania Academy of Fine Arts under Robert Henri while working. He went to Paris for a year in 1895 and then returned to live in New York as a most successful illustrator for the New York *World,* the *Herald, McClure's Magazine, Scribner's,* and the *Saturday Evening Post.* In 1898 he visited Cuba with Luks, and in 1906 he visited France again, as well as Spain. When he re-turned to the United States, Glackens began to devote more time to his painting and was one of the original members of The Eight, or Ashcan School, exhibiting with that group in 1908. Glackens continued to paint in New York until 1925, at which time he returned to France and remained until 1932. His painting during his French years and thereafter shows strong influences of Renoir. Winner of many prizes in his later years, and a skilled observer of the New York scene, Glackens was elected to the National Academy in 1933.

19

PAUL GAUGUIN
French
1848-1903
NAFEA Faa. ipoipo
Rudolf Staechelin Collection, Basle

Paul Gauguin was born in Paris. His father was a journalist and his mother a Peruvian woman from a liberal family. His father died on a trip to Peru when Gauguin was three and he remained in Peru with his mother until the age of seven. He attended boarding school in France until he joined the Merchant Marine, remaining until 1871. Gauguin then became a stockbroker and married the daughter of the Danish Minister to Paris. He painted as a hobby on Sundays and became friendly with Pissarro and other Impressionists, whose work he collected. When he was thirty-five, he gave up his business career to consecrate the rest of his life to painting. In an effort to make enough money to support both his family and himself, he moved to Copenhagen, where he left his wife and family to live on the proceeds of the sale of his collection of paintings. He then returned to France with his eldest son, Clovis, and underwent the worst monetary privations of his life before beginning to sell his own paintings. He made enough money, finally, to send his boy to boarding school and went himself to Pont-Aven in Brittany, to paint. An Impressionist at first, it was after his trip to Martinique in 1887 that Gauguin developed the style known as Synthetism: flat color areas surrounded by heavy black outline, a style deriving from the patterns in cloisonné enamel work. He had his first one-man show in 1888, the year in which he joined van Gogh in Arles. From Arles he again fled to Brittany. By 1891 a lack of success in France and a desire for a more primitive civilization than that of Europe prompted him to go to Tahiti. He remained there until 1893, when ill health and lack of money forced him to leave. He inherited a small sum at this time, but it did not last long and he made up his mind to return permanently to the South Seas. He went back to Tahiti in 1895 and remained on that island until 1901, when, plagued by ill health (his heart was bad) and trouble with the French authorities, he moved to the Marquesas, seeking an easier and cheaper life. His health, unfortunately, deteriorated further and he died of a heart attack in 1903.

GEORGE BENJAMIN LUKS

American

1867-1933

BOY WITH BASEBALL

The Metropolitan Museum of Art, New York
The Edward Joseph Gallagher III Memorial Collection, 1954

George Benjamin Luks was born in Williamsport, Pennsylvania. His father was a doctor and his mother, from whom Luks inherited his ability, was a quite talented amateur painter. He studied first at the Pennsylvania Academy of Fine Arts and then in Düsseldorf, Paris, and London. Upon his return to the United States he became a newspaper illustrator in Philadelphia, where he met Henri, Glackens, Sloan, and Shinn. Sent to Cuba in 1895 to cover an insurrection for his newspaper, Luks was condemned to death, a sentence that luckily was not carried out. After this adventure, he moved to New York to join his friends and to work as an illustrator for the *Tribune* and the *World*. He also painted scenes of coal miners' lives, remembered from his childhood in the Pennsylvania mining district, and New York street scenes. The public received Luks' paintings very poorly and this lack of recognition spurred him on to enter an exhibition in 1908. Luks was active in progressive art movements throughout his life. He also taught—first at the Art Students League, and eventually at his own school. He was the recipient of many awards, including the Medal of the Art Institute of Chicago in 1920 and 1926 and the Corcoran Gold Medal in 1933.

21

VINCENT van GOGH
Dutch
1853-1890
GARDENING PATCHES ON MONTMARTRE IN WINTER
Collection of V. W. van Gogh, Stedelijk Museum, Amsterdam

Vincent van Gogh was born at Groot-Zundest, Holland. His father was a pastor and two of his uncles were art dealers. Vincent began his career at the age of sixteen as an art salesman in Goupil's gallery in The Hague, where he began his letters to his devoted and beloved brother, Theo. From The Hague, Vincent was sent to a branch of the gallery in London, and then, in 1875, to another in Paris. This happy period when he was absorbed by the life around him ended abruptly when his work was found unsatisfactory. A short while later, back in Holland, van Gogh decided to become a lay preacher and eventually went to work as a missionary in the Borinage, a dreary, poverty-stricken mining district in Belgium. There he behaved like a saint, depriving himself of life's necessities, and found himself dismissed for over-zealousness. He remained in Belgium to study art, determined to give happiness by creating beauty. His first important work, *The Potato Eaters,* was painted in 1885. In 1886 he joined his brother Theo, now manager of Goupil's in Paris. Vincent went to study with Cormon and met Pissarro, Monet, and Gauguin; he began to lighten his very somber palette and to paint in the short brush-strokes of the Impressionists. His life was comparatively happy, but his nervous temperament made him a difficult companion. In addition, discussions at night and painting by day undermined his health and he decided to go south to find a more congenial atmosphere for painting. He settled on Arles, hoping that his friends would join him and help found a school of art. Gauguin did, with disastrous results. In a fit of epilepsy, van Gogh pursued his friend with an open razor, was stopped by Gauguin's icy look, and cut off his own ear. He began to alternate between fits of madness and more lucid periods and was sent to the asylum at Saint-Rémy for treatment. By May of 1890 he seemed much better and it was decided that he go to Auvers-sur-Oise, near Paris, to be watched over by Dr. Gachet. Although this relationship was a good one and Vincent's works at Auvers were remarkably fine, his mind deteriorated still further, and on a July day he shot himself in the chest, dying two days later. Even at the end, van Gogh's thoughts showed his love of humanity. "I did it for the good of all," he told his brother.

22
HENRI MATISSE
French

1869-1954

PLUM BLOSSOMS, GREEN BACKGROUND

Collection of Mrs. Albert D. Lasker, New York

Henri Matisse was born in Le Cateau. His father was a grain merchant and his mother a quite talented amateur painter. Matisse was studying law and working as a lawyer's clerk when he fell ill. By chance, during his convalescence he read a book entitled *How to Paint*. From that moment on he was lost to the law profession and finally persuaded his father to let him study art in Paris. Matisse was then only twenty-one. He studied at the Académie Julian, then at the Beaux-Arts, and then copied old masters in the Louvre. He discovered Impressionism in 1898, and then the works of the Divisionists and Cézanne. By 1905 he was the leader of the Fauves, but three years later he had already begun to paint in pure, clear color.

Travel to the south of France and to Morocco further stimulated his use of color and pattern and the development of his use of color for modeling and giving substance. Matisse's reputation was worldwide by 1918 and he had many commissions for book illustrations, ballet sets, and murals. His most famous mural is *La Danse,* done for the Barnes Foundation in Philadelphia. His last great public work was the complete decoration—stained glass, furniture, murals, and chasubles —for the Dominican Chapel in Vence, a work done only in tones of ochre, black, and white. In the last years of his life Matisse created cut-paper paintings in brilliant combinations of color. He died in Vence after a full, fruitful life in the fall of 1954.

23

HENRI de TOULOUSE-LAUTREC
French
1864-1901
PROFILE D'UNE FEMME
Musée du Louvre, Paris

Count Henri de Toulouse-Lautrec was born in Albi in one of the castles of his ancestors, the Counts of Toulouse. He was a delicate child, but led a normal life until he was fourteen. Then, in minor accidents, he broke first one thighbone and then the other. The bones did not heal properly due to a rare bone disease and when, finally, he could walk again, he had a normal torso but abnormally stunted legs. Since he had shown talent in drawing as a very young child, his parents encouraged him to take lessons with various teachers in Paris. When he was twenty, his father provided a financial arrangement which enabled Lautrec to set up his own studio on the rue Caulaincourt in Montmartre. He frequented Impressionist circles and particularly admired Degas. Between 1887 and 1897, Lautrec produced the best and greatest part of his work. He painted, sketched, made lithographs and posters, and illustrated books. His production was enormous, for he worked feverishly, as if he knew that his days were numbered. His ill-

ness began to affect his brain in 1898, and his family sent him to a private asylum for treatment. While shut away he worked on a series of circus drawings, which were instrumental in securing his release, for the doctors recognized that they were the work of a sane man. For a short while his health, somewhat improved by care and rest, was good enough for him to return to his studio and to work. However, in the spring of 1901 he became partially paralyzed. He was taken to one of his family's estates at Malromé, where he died a few months later.

Profile of a Woman is a sketch in chalk, much more acid and biting in style than his other portraits. This woman is revealed as dignified and full of character, but she is a bit hard and Lautrec has used a heavier line to indicate this. Lightning-quick, Impressionistic strokes are used sparingly on the dark oatmeal paper to indicate highlights in blue and white, giving a brilliant effect.

24
PIERRE BONNARD
French
1867-1947
BOUQUET DE FLEURS
Besson Collection

Pierre Bonnard was born in Fontenay-aux-Roses not far from Paris. A law student before he transferred to the Beaux-Arts, Bonnard later attended the Académie Julian, where he met Denis, Sérusier, and Vuillard, among others, and with whom he was associated in about 1891 in the group known as the *Nabis* (Prophets). Bonnard was the "Japanese" Nabi because of his interest in Gauguin and Japanese prints relayed to the group by Sérusier who had been at Pont-Aven. Sharing a studio with Vuillard, Denis, and Lugné-Poë, the theatrical producer, Bonnard's earliest works were theatrical sets, furniture decorations, screens, and posters. He contributed regularly to *La Revue Blanche,* a periodical, and made a set of lithographs based on aspects of life in Paris for Ambroise Vollard, as well as illustrations for books. By 1896, at his first exhibition, it was clear that Bonnard was the painter who could bring magic to the simplest things in life: bathtubs, women, children, gardens, and the sea. Like Vuillard, with whom he was always closely linked, he was an "intimist", a painter constantly delighted by the most ordinary objects and actions to which he brought a constant freshness. Bonnard was attracted by the color of the Impressionists, but unlike them he was not so dazzled by color as to forget form and reality, and he worked much more slowly to capture on canvas his own rebellion against current styles of art and pre-decided theories. Bonnard's palette was exquisite: rainbow-like, pearly in flesh-tones, with shadows ranging from pinks, blues, golds to opaque grays or deep blues. His paintings transpose solids and transparencies, light and shade, and have an abstract structural quality that is both decorative and satisfying in its use of space, foreshadowing the works of Matisse. From his paintings, still-lifes, landscapes, and figures, emerges the artist who looked at the world around him with as much joy when an old man as a youth, the artist whose perception stayed keen, and whose vision remained so personal and immutably honest.

MARY CASSATT

American

1845-1927

AFTER THE BATH

The Cleveland Museum of Art, Ohio

Mary Cassatt was born in Pittsburgh. The daughter of a millionaire, she spent her childhood abroad with her family. Some time after the Cassatts' return to live in Philadelphia, Mary studied at the Pennsylvania Academy of Fine Arts; by the time she was twenty-three she had decided, against her father's wishes, to return to Europe for further study. She went to Italy, Spain, and Belgium, and finally to Paris where, as she has said, the sight of pastel by Degas changed her life. She became Degas' pupil and through him joined the Impressionist group. Her works were accepted at first by the official Salons, but after rejections in 1875 and 1877 she showed only with the Impressionists. Cassatt worked in oils and pastels and also made etchings and lithographs. In all of her work may be seen the influence of Degas and of Japanese prints, but she was very original in her use of color and her handling of themes, using strong, sure line. Although she was successful in France, she was not recognized in her own country until 1892, when she was commissioned to paint one wall of the Woman's Building at the Chicago Exposition. She received the French Légion d'Honneur in 1904. After 1914 her sight began to fail, and she could no longer work. She remained in France until her death in 1926. Mary Cassatt never married, but some of her natural maternal instinct found an outlet in her many paintings of women and children.

26

CLAUDE MONET

French

1840-1926

ROUGH SEA AT ETRETAT

Musée du Louvre, Paris

Claude Monet was born in Paris, but spent his childhood and youth in Le Havre, where he began his career by drawing caricatures and later studying with Boudin. He went to study at the Académie Gleyre in 1860 and there met Renoir, Sisley, and Bazille. By 1870, when the Franco-Prussian War broke out, the four had begun to formulate their own ideas on painting. Monet and Sisley fled to England, where they saw the works of Turner and Constable and crystallized their own theories. In 1872 Monet was at Argenteuil, where he set up his studio on a boat and began to put his ideas on canvas. From the famous First Impressionist Exhibition in 1874 to the end of his long life, Monet never ceased to be an Impressionist, although in his final years his works take on a drowned look and approach abstract expressionism. Success came late to Monet, and it was not until 1891 that he could purchase the house he had rented in Giverny some eight years earlier. He then constructed an Impressionistic garden including a riot of loose color and overflowing flower beds, a lily pond ,and a Japanese boathouse. Sitting in a small boat in his lily pond, he painted his famous *Water Lily* series, showing the pond in all seasons and at all hours of the day from early dawn to twilight.

ODILON REDON
French
1840-1916
VASE OF FLOWERS
Musée du Louvre, Paris

Odilon Redon was born in Bordeaux. When he was seven, his parents took him to Paris so that he might visit the Louvre. The experience made such a mark upon the boy that by the time he was fifteen he had made up his mind to become an artist. He began by studying watercolor painting, at the same time studying botany, for he had met the botanist Clavaud, who stimulated in him an interest in nature that was to influence his entire life. After studying architecture in Bordeaux during the year 1857, Redon went to Paris to study painting with Gérôme, an experience that would have discouraged him had he not met Besnard, the etcher, who encouraged and instructed him in that medium. In 1870 Redon settled in Montparnasse. His most intimate friends there were Corot, Cour-bet, and Fantin-Latour. The latter profoundly influenced Redon, and the two men visited the Louvre together to study the works of the old masters. Fantin-Latour also gave Redon his first lessons in lithography. Redon's first collection of lithographs, *In the Dream,* appeared when the artist was forty. His work was barely noticed until the newer and younger generation of artists and writers, led by Gauguin and Huysmans, took notice of Redon's delicate and dreamy, sometimes quite Surrealistic, work. His success came late, but it was widespread and solid, and gave Redon what he had always wanted. He bought a small house in the country near Paris in 1909 and retired to lead a quiet life of meditation, reading, studying botany, and painting until his death in 1916.

28

PIERRE AUGUSTE RENOIR

French

1841-1919

GIRL WITH WATERING CAN

National Gallery of Art, Washington, D.C.
Chester Dale Collection

Pierre Auguste Renoir was born in Limoges. As a boy, he was a painter's apprentice in a porcelain factory. When he was twenty-one he went to Paris and studied at the Académie Gleyre with Monet, Sisley, and Bazille. The four young men painted together in Fontainebleau Forest and at Asnières and Argenteuil. When the Franco-Prussian War broke out in 1870, Renoir and Bazille joined the French Army. Bazille was killed in a cavalry charge in 1871; thus the future Impressionist group lost one of its most promising painters. Renoir, the first of the Impressionists to achieve success, exhibited with his friends until 1879, at which time he came to feel that Impressionism held no more for him. He then traveled to Italy and in 1883 worked with Cézanne at L'Estaque. For a very short period his work became dry and almost academic, but by 1885 he had found his own style in which color and form fuse into a mov-ing luminous mass. Renoir began to suffer from arthritis in 1889. After spending several winters on the French Riviera, he finally settled in Cagnes. By 1912, his arms and legs almost completely para-lyzed, he worked with brushes strapped to his wrists, sitting in a wheelchair with his palette on his knees. He continued to paint until the day of his death in 1919.

Renoir's paintings glorify women. He loved their beauty and their gentleness, their laughter and their gravity, their tenderness and their co-quetry. He painted women indoors and out; in public places and at home; tending their children; reading; sewing; doing chores; admiring them-selves innocently as they try on hats, pose flowers in their hair, and pin on jewels. He painted them singly or in groups, in elegant robes or simple dresses, and they are always perfectly lovely, per-fectly natural, and always perfectly understood.

29

HENRI ROUSSEAU (Le Douanier)

French

1844-1910

ENVIRONS OF PARIS

The Cleveland Museum of Art, Ohio

Henri Rousseau was born in Laval, the son of a tinker. After the usual elementary schooling, he entered the army and served as a saxophonist in the band. His claim to have been sent to Mexico with the forces of Napoleon III is discounted entirely by French biographers, but is accepted by others at its face value. He became a minor customs official in 1869, after working as a lawyer's clerk. He took part in the Franco-Prussian War and at its close was appointed to a customs post in Paris. By the time he was forty, he was able to retire on a very small pension, which he supplemented by giving lessons in music, elocution, and painting. He also painted portraits of neighborhood shopkeepers, measuring them with a tape-measure before beginning to draw. His work attracted the attention of many journalists and noted painters—Gauguin, Redon, Pissarro, and Seurat, among others—and he was invited to exhibit with the Independents in 1886. He continued to show at this Salon until

1910. Entirely self-taught, Rousseau was as delightful a personality as he was a painter. He gave little evening parties at which his pupils performed, sending out hand-printed invitations that were eagerly accepted by Parisian artists. In 1908 the artists returned the compliment by giving him a huge party in Picasso's studio in the rue Ravignan. His last years of life were clouded by his arrest for fraud, for he had been taken advantage of by a swindler. Rousseau was fined, but his one-year sentence was suspended on the grounds that he was a first offender and so naïve that he could believe anything. In 1910 he injured a leg, neglected the wound, which became gangrenous, and died in the hospital in September of that year. Although only seven people attended his funeral, as his artist friends were all away from Paris, he received the later homage of a tombstone designed by Robert Delaunay and an epitaph by Apollinaire; a most fitting tribute to a fine painter.

30

EDOUARD MANET

French

1832-1883

THE FIFER

Musée du Louvre, Paris

Edouard Manet was born in Paris, where his father was a governmental official. Even though he showed early artistic talent, Edouard seemed destined for the Navy until he failed the Naval examinations. Then his father permitted him to study art with Couture. But such academic instruction did not satisfy Manet and he began to study the old masters by himself and to travel abroad to see more of their works. Some of his early paintings were shown at the regular Salons, but in 1863 his *Déjeuner sur l'herbe* at the Salon des Refusés created a scandal and Manet was bitterly criticized and accused of inciting younger artists to revolt against the established order. Although Manet painted in sharp contrasts of light and dark, and in broad planes and color areas, he influenced the Impressionists enormously. A traditional Realist, he nevertheless painted Impressionistic harbor and water scenes, used a varied palette, and, most important, painted scenes of contemporary life. Manet developed a form of progressive paralysis at the age of forty-eight. After years of suffering and futile treatment, ending in the amputation of a foot, he died at the age of fifty-one.

The Fifer, a work painted in 1866, is so simple in appearance as to be completely deceptive. The color areas are large and limited mostly to red and black. The background, like those of Velasquez, is monochromatic pale olive. There is no shadow at all in this painting. A dark line encircling the entire subject rounds out the figure, makes the colors vibrate, and imparts solidity and life. The boy is not a cardboard figure but a breathing human being. Only the hand of a master such as Manet, so deft and sure, could have created this painting.

31

EDGAR DEGAS

French

1834-1917

DANCER ON STAGE

Musée du Louvre, Paris

Edgar Degas, the son of an aristocratic banker, was born in Paris. After the customary schooling he began the study of law; however, he soon defied his father's wishes and entered the Ecole des Beaux-Arts at the age of twenty-one. A year later he went to Italy and studied the art of the Middle Ages and the Renaissance, as he had previously studied that of Clouet and Poussin at the Louvre. Upon his return to Paris in 1861, he met Manet and a group of younger artists and began to paint scenes of racetracks; he made sketches at the track but completed his works from wooden models in his studio. He served in the National Guard in the War of 1870, went to New Orleans in 1872, and upon his return to Paris, widened his choice of subjects to include dancers, café scenes, and contemporary life in general. Degas exhibited with the Impressionists until 1879 as an important member of the group; after that he limited the number of works he showed to as few as five. Between 1873 and 1883 he produced the bulk of his work and perfected his technique of working in layers of pastels. His application of as many as six fixed successive layers, plus a seventh unfixed, imparted a powdery effect. As he grew older, he grew more and more misogynistic and seclusive, and his eyesight, about which he had complained for years, grew steadily worse. He roamed about the streets of Paris, unhappy and alone in his last years, and died in 1917.

Degas' dancers—there are hundreds of them, in oils, pastels, tempera, gouache, charcoal and pencil—are revelations of human movement, unstudied, often awkward or embarrassing, but always accurate. He catches his subjects as if with a camera, but adds to the present moment a hint of what has gone before and then, what will follow.

32

PAUL CEZANNE
French
1839-1906
THE KITCHEN TABLE
Musée du Louvre, Paris

Paul Cézanne was born in Aix-en-Provence. His father, a banker, wished his son to study law, but finally agreed to let him study art in Paris and provided him with a small allowance. Cézanne, through Emile Zola, with whom he had gone to school in Aix, met the Impressionists Pissarro and Guillaumin. He studied at the Académie Suisse, but failed the entrance examination to the Beaux-Arts and returned home, discouraged. However, he went back to Paris again, determined to paint, and for a time worked fairly closely with Manet, Renoir, and Degas. After the Franco-Prussian War, when he was thirty-two, Cézanne began to develop his own theory of painting and his own style, based on the reduction of every object in nature to the cube, the cylinder, and the cone, and on the use of color for modeling and imparting solidity and perspective. Between 1872 and 1888 Cézanne divided his time between Paris and Aix. In 1890 he was stricken with diabetes and retired to Aix to live. By this time his father had died, leaving Cézanne a large fortune which made him financially independent of his lack of success. In-

deed, it was not until 1895 that he began to receive the recognition he deserved for his revolutionary ideas, which have affected all painting since his own time. Cézanne was determined to die painting and he did. Seven days before his death, out on a painting trip, he was caught in a downpour and had to be brought home in a farm cart. He recovered enough to go out into his garden to paint once again and died at his easel, in October 1906.

Cézanne conceived his paintings intellectually and none of his work is the result of accident. He painted and repainted, altered brush strokes, arranged and rearranged, made innumerable sketches and drawings, sometimes attacked his subjects from several angles in the same canvas, required his human sitters to pose interminably, propped up fruits, and tilted bottles and baskets. The results are serenity, the fixation of time, landscapes of enduring beauty, and solidity of objects and bodies. Cézanne captures a moment in eternity, the moment he deliberately chose as representative of everything that he wished to convey.

33

LUC-ALBERT MOREAU

French

1882-1948

KNOCKOUT

Musée du Louvre, Paris

Luc-Albert Moreau was born in Paris. He originally intended to study law and began his career as a lawyer's clerk, working during the day and studying Asiatic and African languages at night. He had received a diploma from the School of Oriental Languages when, in 1906, he decided to study art and began to attend, somewhat irregularly, the Académie Julian and other Paris art schools. He first exhibited his paintings in 1908 and continued to paint until the outbreak of war in 1914. He was mobilized as a machine-gunner and, by the time he was badly wounded at Compiègne in 1918, he was an infantry lieutenant. Moreau had painted and sketched throughout his military service. When the war ended, he received the Croix de Guerre and was made a Chevalier of the Legion of Honor. In 1919 he became vice-president of the Society of Independent Artists. Moreau continued to paint until his death, but is best known in France for his World War I drawings and paintings.

Knockout concentrates its interest on the loneliness of the beaten and exhausted boxer's defeat. The composition adds to the loneliness of the subject's abandoned pose. The ring seems enormous and empty; the cheering is somewhere else and we see only the magnificent body in its prone and helpless position, still full of life. A profound humanity and deep understanding is evident in this capably painted and intensely moving work.

34

EUGENE BOUDIN

French

1824-1898

BATHERS ON THE TROUVILLE BEACH

Musée du Louvre, Paris

Eugène Boudin was born in Honfleur in 1824, the son of a fisherman and a stewardess. He began working as a cabin boy at the age of ten, but fell overboard one day and his mother decided that he would have to work on land. When his family moved to Le Havre, Boudin went to work as a printer's clerk and later became a salesman in an art-supply store. Millet bought his paints in the shop and gave Boudin some advice on his drawing, the only formal art training Boudin ever received. For a short while, he was part owner of an art-supply store. After quarrelling with his partner in 1846, he devoted all of his time to painting and by 1852 had an exhibition in Le Havre. Boudin introduced Monet to the delights of painting in the open air, thus foreshadowing the work of the Impressionist school. Among other friends and admirers of Boudin were Corot, Courbet, Sisley, Puvis de Chavannes, Manet, and Jongkind. He made his Paris debut in 1859, showing each year at the official Salons. He received a third-class medal in 1881, and the Legion of Honor in 1892. Boudin was very little appreciated by the general public in his lifetime and died, comparatively poor, in 1898.

Boudin, as might be expected, was primarily a painter of marine scenes. Courbet called him a "seraph" and the "only one who understood the sky." Boudin's paintings and drawings are always two-thirds sky and one-third water or beach.

35

WILLIAM ROBINSON LEIGH
American
1866-1955
RETURN OF THE WAR CANOES
The Rockwell Gallery, Corning, New York

William Robinson Leigh was born in Berkeley County, West Virginia. He attended the Maryland Institute of Art before going to Munich where he studied under several nature painters for twelve years and won two medals. Leigh also exhibited at the Salon of Paris in 1892 and gained an Honorable Mention. He returned to the United States shortly after and took up residence in Brooklyn, New York, but his dearest wish was to paint the West in the manner he had learned in Munich. As he himself described this in his later years, this was to "start with a detailed charcoal drawing and then paint over that—the most distant things first. If there are no clouds, the sky may take more than a day. The distant figures may be done in a week. It gets more difficult as you approach the foreground—a large canvas may take four to six months

altogether—but the most economical way is to finish as you go." It was not until 1906 when he was forty that he managed to persuade the Santa Fe Railroad to give him a free ticket in exchange for a painting of the Grand Canyon. The company gave him five more commissions when the first painting was completed. For the rest of his life, Leigh rode about the West on horseback, sketching as he went, and then returning to his studio to complete commissions. His works are full of lively movement, bright in color, with a feeling for the vanished past that is quite unequalled. Bright sunshine, clean, clear air, and the smell of the golden dust emanate from his works while the soundness of his academic training and his painstaking methods permitted the achievement of a highly exact realism in his often exciting scenes.

36

JOHN SINGER SARGENT
American
1856-1925
THE OYSTER GATHERERS OF CANCALE
The Corcoran Gallery of Art, Washington, D.C.

John Singer Sargent, the celebrated international portraitist, was born in Florence, Italy. His parents were American and his mother, a Philadelphian, had a passion for travel. The Sargent family spent their lives in hotels and rented houses, in every place but home. Sargent's mother was also interested in painting and it was she who led her son to the art. He began his formal training in Paris at the age of nineteen, studying with Carolus-Duran, a French academic painter then very popular. Sargent remained with Duran from 1874 to 1876 and emerged from his studies with a completely finished technique and style. He then travelled, finally seeing the United States at the age of twenty, returning to Europe to visit Spain where he admired the portraits of Velasquez, and going to North Africa where he made brilliant water-color sketches of the landscape, before opening a studio in Paris in 1881. In 1884, he painted the portrait known as *Madame X* and exhibited it at the Salon where it was greeted with horror for its realism by the critics and the public and with hysterics on the part of the sitter, Madame Gautreau, a professional beauty who was as egoistic, vain, daring in dress, and sickly as Sargent indicates. Sargent, who had received nothing but praise before this, left Paris for London which he made his permanent headquarters, and the point to which he returned from his travels devoted to painting the wealthy and powerful international set. Sargent's technique was brilliant. He was able to paint texture of fabrics, skin tones, color, and shape in an iridescent surface shimmer, recording forever a way of life and a superficial society that has now vanished completely. Now, fifty or more years later, the surface brilliance of the portraits matches in our eyes a brilliantly surfaced and shallow society. Sargent's water-colors and oils have more reality than his portraits and his desire to be a fully-rounded artist may be noted in murals based on symbolic and religious subjects painted for the Boston Museum and the Boston Library.

37

WINSLOW HOMER
American
1836-1910

SNAP THE WHIP
The Butler Institute of American Art, Youngstown, Ohio

Winslow Homer was born in Boston. He had no formal art training beyond apprenticeship to a lithographer, but by the time he was twenty-one he was employed as an illustrator by *Harper's Weekly,* a career that he continued until 1875. He moved to New York in 1859, worked by day at his illustrating, and took night courses at the National Academy of Design. In 1862 *Harper's* sent him to cover the Civil War and Homer did his first oil painting. The first public recognition he received as a painter came in 1866 for a work called *Prisoners at the Front.* After the war, Homer began a series of typical *genre* works and made enough money to go to France for about a year. When he returned to the United States, he continued his work as a book- and magazine-illustrator and also painted farm scenes, children, and Negro subjects. He went to England in 1881 and painted watercolors of the sea at Tynemouth. Two years later he settled in Prout's Neck, Maine, and began his long series of sea studies, which was continued at Nassau, in the Bahamas, where he spent his winters. At first his paintings of the sea included human figures, but gradually the sea and the force of nature became the only subjects of these works. For the rest of his life he traveled and painted, going as far north as Canada and as far south as the West Indies, always taking instruction from nature.

38

FREDERIC REMINGTON

American
1861-1909

THE APACHE

The Rockwell Gallery, Corning, New York

Frederic Remington was born in Canton, New York, the son of a newspaper editor who moved to Ogdensburg shortly after the boy's birth. Remington attended both the Yale Art School and the New York Art Students League before going West. Although he had already decided, at the age of nineteen, that he wished to be an artist, he worked as a cowboy and a scout, ran a sheep and mule ranch, went broke, and was helped home by a friend. He then visited Germany, Russia, and North Africa. Upon his return to the United States, he became an artist and correspondent in Cuba during the Spanish-American War. Then, his adventures over, he settled down in New Rochelle, New York, to paint, sculpt, and illustrate books. About six months after he moved to Ridgefield, Connecticut, his career was cut short by a fatal attack of appendicitis.

Remington's works are extremely realistic and often depict scenes of violence and warfare. Action is swift and details of country and costume are accurate. When he drew or painted, he distinguished clearly between a Sioux and an Apache, a stand of sage and a clump of cactus. *The Apache* stirs the imagination with its feeling of imminent danger while it delights the eye with its bright golden atmosphere. It recalls, in its background color, such childhood favorites as *Riders of the Purple Sage,* and adds visual imagery to the history of the warfare of the plains and the heritage of the west.

39
JAMES ABBOTT McNEILL WHISTLER
American
1834-1903
PORTRAIT OF THE ARTIST'S MOTHER
Musée du Louvre, Paris

Whistler was born in Lowell, Massachusetts, a fact of which he did not care to be reminded. His father was a builder of railroads and took his son, then aged nine, with him to St. Petersburg, where he lived like an aristocrat and attended the Russian Academy of Fine Arts. When her husband died, Whistler's mother refused to have her son join the Czar's household as an imperial page and brought him back to Massachusetts. Young Whistler was appalled by the countrified atmosphere of the family farm and successively: flunked out of West Point, gave up a job in a locomotive works to work for the U.S. Coastal Geodetic Service, and read Murger's *La Vie de Bohème*. That convinced him that Paris was the place for him and he left the United States in 1855, never to return. He studied with Gleyre in Paris, met Manet, Monet, and Degas, exhibited in the 1863 Salon des Refusés,

and then inexplicably travelled to South America before finally settling in London. Whistler was quite successful as an artist in England and even more successful as a sharp-tongued wit. However, he was forced into bankruptcy after winning a notorious lawsuit against John Ruskin, the English critic, since the lawsuit damaged his own reputation. He returned to live in Paris in 1890, opened a school of art, and died there in 1903. He painted very little in his last years and owes his final artistic success to his famous etchings.

Whistler is best known for his famous portrait of his mother. His paintings, although Impressionistic in their use of harmonies in greys, blacks, and whites, remain outside the general trend of that school and are quite individualistic, showing great technical skill and knowledge of his subjects.

40

THOMAS EAKINS

American

1844-1916

MAX SCHMITT IN A SINGLE SCULL

The Metropolitan Museum of Art, New York
Alfred N. Punnett Endowment Fund and Gift of George D. Pratt, 1934

Thomas Eakins was a native Philadelphian. After studying the making of antique casts at the Pennsylvania Academy of Fine Arts and anatomy at the Jefferson Medical College, he went to Paris in 1866. He studied at the Ecole des Beaux-Arts under Gérôme and Bonnat but, finding classical form and academic style not to his liking, went to Spain to study the works of Velasquez and Ribera. He returned to the United States in 1870 and worked as a portraitist. To add to his income, he became an instructor in anatomy and life classes at the Pennsylvania Academy in 1876. He was forced to resign ten years later because of the scandal that occurred when he posed a nude model before a mixed class. He continued to do *genre* pictures and to paint portraits of his family and close friends but had very little success. He became more and more of a recluse, although he continued to teach anatomy at the National Academy of Design in New York and even won a few prizes. From 1910 until his death in 1916, he was in failing health and painted very little.

Eakins was a realist with great technical skill. Never sentimental, either in style or choice of subjects, he wanted only to paint American life as he saw it, without resorting to any romanticism.

41
ALFRED SISLEY
French
1839-1899
L'INONDATION A PORT-MARLY
Musée du Louvre, Paris

Alfred Sisley was born in France of English parents. He studied at the Académie Gleyre with Renoir, Monet, and Bazille and took part with them in the informal evening discussions at the Café Guerbois. As an Englishman, he was the mediator between the rival factions: Manet and Degas versus Monet and Renoir. Café life is a unique French cultural phenomenon and continues there today. People come and go as they please; discussion is open to all; writers and artists exchange ideas on all subjects, criticize, formulate theories, and stimulate each other. After the 1863 Salon des Refusés, Sisley and Monet left Paris to live in the still-rural suburbs and to paint landscapes. As a young man, Sisley was well supplied with money by his father, but the War of 1870 and subsequent panics ruined the family business. After his return from England in 1872, Sisley knew great poverty, which continued throughout most of his career. Even when his works began to sell in 1876, they brought very modest sums. He died of throat cancer at the age of sixty in Moret-sur-Loing, a beautiful little town that reveres his name and points with great pride to the scenes he immortalized in his many works.

Sisley's landscapes are poetic in quality and have a great reticent, underlying emotion. *L'Inondation à Port-Marly* is one of several works painted after a serious flood at Port-Marly, near St. Germain-en-Laye. Here, as in many of his works, color is stronger in the foreground than in the background—a technique that adds perspective and depth to the canvas. Impressionistic in technique, sensitive in feeling, and beautiful to look at, the landscape is also solidly realistic. The artist is as aware of the disaster's effects upon the inhabitants of the village as he is of the beauty of the sun on the water and the freshly washed trees. But the artist has time to see this beauty, while the men in the small boats have time only for rescue missions.

42

CAMILLE PISSARRO
French
1830-1903
IN THE GARDEN
Narodni Galerie, Prague

Camille Pissarro was born on St. Thomas, Virgin Islands. As a boy, he was sent to school in France. Although his love of drawing manifested itself early and he was encouraged by his French instructors to pursue this field, he returned to St. Thomas to work for five years in his father's business. At twenty-two, after he ran away to Caracas with a Danish painter, his parents finally agreed to his return to Paris to study art. He arrived in France when he was twenty-five, and attended the Ecole des Beaux-Arts and then the Académie Suisse, where he met Cézanne. Cézanne introduced him to Monet and the other Impressionists. Pissarro, ten years older than the others, became their informal leader, giving them advice and set-

tling their disputes. Only happy when living in the country, he moved to Pontoise to raise his family, struggling desperately in doing so. An early convert to Impressionism, he painted in this manner all of his life except for a brief period between 1885 and 1890. At this time, having met Seurat, he experimented briefly with Pointillism, which he eventually discovered was "not for him." Comparative success came very late to Pissarro and it was not until 1891, thirty-six years after he had begun his career, that he was able to travel a little and to buy the small house in Eragny in which he lived. His sight began to fail in his last years, and he painted a series of street scenes viewed through his closed windows just before his death in 1903.

43

KAWANABE KYOSAI
Japanese
1831-1889
TIGER
Collection of Samuel Shore, New York

Kawanabe Kyosai was, when little more than a boy, a pupil of Kuniyoshi. However, his main training came from a Kano artist, Tohaku. Kyosai was well known for his lively spirit of fun and is said to have lived a riotous life, doing his best work under the influence of *sake*. Few painters have had so much ability to portray such vivid action.

This lean and obviously hungry tiger is stalking his prey. His yellow eyes gleam with ferocity and his pelt bristles with rage, its orange, black, and white gleaming against a pale grey background. The realism of *Tiger* is so strong that the viewer almost expects the beast to keep walking, right off the paper into the room to claim his next victim.

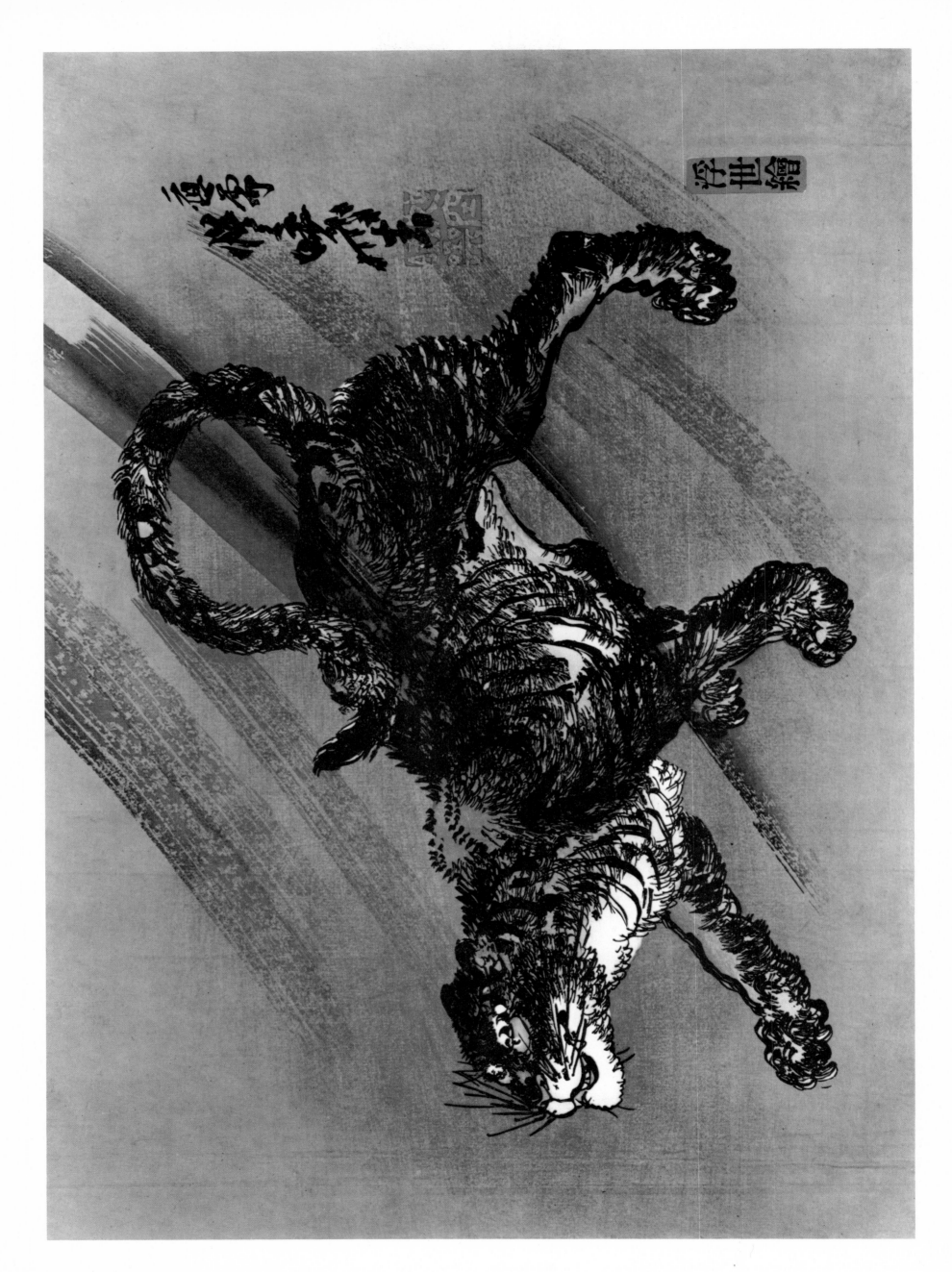

44

GEORGE INNESS

American

1825-1894

THE COMING STORM

Addison Gallery of American Art, Phillips Academy,
Andover, Massachusetts

George Inness was born in Newburgh, New York, a town on the Hudson River. His family soon moved to Newark, New Jersey, and George worked as a grocery clerk before getting a better job with a map-making firm. Self-taught at first, he began painting in 1841 and had a successful exhibition at the National Academy of Design in 1845. He then went abroad to study but followed no particular school, although he favored the work of Constable and Corot. A nervous man who had been epileptic as a child, he had strange methods of working because he found it difficult to begin a painting. But once he had put down one shape, his imagination leaped ahead. It is said that his fellow artists hid their works when he came to visit, as he was otherwise liable to develop the creative process they had begun, changing everything on the canvas. Inness lived in New York and Massa-chusetts and travelled to California and Yosemite. Elected to the National Academy in 1868, he did not become financially secure until 1875, when Thomas B. Clarke became his patron. He was then able to concentrate on developing his ability, with no further anxiety, until his death in 1894.

The Coming Storm illustrates Inness' romantic and mystic approach to nature. The canvas has a feeling of strength and power and shows a broad sweep of rich countryside. The land is peaceful and life upon it is slow. The cows graze undisturbed and the farmer moves from one chore to another unhurriedly. The golden color is that of a late summer day. And overhead, in dramatic contrast, storm clouds pile up in the sky, grey and white and unheeded, so that we can almost smell the coming rain, the renewal of an ageless cycle.

45

ALBERT BIERSTADT
American
1830-1902

THE ROCKY MOUNTAINS

The Metropolitan Museum of Art, New York
Rogers Fund, 1907

Albert Bierstadt, the leading painter of what may be called the Rocky Mountain section of the Hudson River school, was born near Düsseldorf in Germany. He came to the United States in 1832 and spent his boyhood in Massachusetts, at first showing no signs of interest in painting. He produced his first oil when he was twenty-one and two years later went back to Düsseldorf to remain for four years, learning to paint in the approved 19th-century German Romantic manner. Biersadt returned to America in 1857 and spent a summer in the White Mountains of New Hampshire to sketch and take photographs of scenery. In 1858, he joined a government expedition to the Rocky Mountains where he made quick sketches in oil, never taking more than fifteen minutes for a scene. His aim was to rework these sketches in his studio to get the best effects possible from the picturesque and unknown scenery. Since he was not interested in exactitude, he altered the scenery for dramatic weight and thus distinguished himself from the meticulously naturalistic Hudson River artists:

Cole, Church, and Durand. Bierstadt's works are dramatically lighted and colored almost to a formula, ice-blue water, richly green foregrounds sharply distinguished from blue and green mountains, fading hazily into the distance and capped with fluffy clouds making bright reflections. Genre elements—animals, Indians, soldiers, people—were placed in the immediate foreground. Both as original oils and as engravings, Bierstadt's works were very successful both in the United States where the romantic West opened up a new frontier and in Europe where his works fortified the conception of the wildness of the country. Before long, he was commanding prices up to $35,000 for a large oil and his works adorned castles of Europe and American millionaires' homes. European critics understood his work and he was awarded medals in Austria, Prussia, Bavaria, Belgium, and France. He chose, however, to live in the United States and built a huge castle, Malkasten, overlooking the Hudson, in which he lived and worked until death, surrounded by trophies of the hunt.

46

WORTHINGTON WHITTREDGE
American
1820-1910
TROUT BROOK
The Corcoran Gallery of Art, Washington, D.C.

Worthington Whittredge was born in a log cabin near Springfield, Ohio. Before he was twenty-three he had worked as a farm-hand, been a sign painter's apprentice, failed as a commercial photographer and given up itinerant portrait painting. The chance to study Hudson River landscapes in Cincinnati convinced him that his interest lay in landscape painting in hilly country. Whittredge went to Europe in 1849, paying his way with commissions to be executed abroad. He remained for ten years, visiting England, Belgium, the Barbizon School in France, and then spending four years in Düsseldorf, where he learned to paint in a manner that he had later to discard. He next passed five years in Italy sketching in the summers and painting landscapes to sell to tourists in the winters. Whittredge returned to the United States in 1859 and settled in New York City, although his connections were all in Ohio. It was then that Whittredge discovered that the brazen palette he

had acquired in Germany ruined his views of the American forests. In 1865 he travelled with John Kensett, a Hudson River artist, and Sanford Gifford, a minor member of the same group, to the Rocky Mountains. Whittredge was most impressed by the vast, stretching plains, and under the influence of Kensett began to coordinate what he had learned abroad with what was most suitable in his own country. His palette became gentler and more poetic, his compositions emphasized horizontals with far-off mountains closing in the backgrounds and achieved a pictorial representation of wide-stretching space, while his short, rapid brush strokes caused details to vanish as the viewer approached the painting. Whittredge's harmonious mature style is calm, quiet, and lyrical. When he returned to the East, using naturalistic tonal variations in his paintings of sunlit forests, stone walls, old houses, and naked dunes, he indicated lovingly that which was already old in the New World.

47

GUSTAVE COURBET

French

1819-1877

THE CLIFF AT ETRETAT AFTER THE STORM

Musée du Louvre, Paris

Gustave Courbet was born in Ornans in the Franche-Comté, the son of a comfortable family, half-peasant, half-bourgeois, and very proud of its revolutionary ancestry. Courbet, a handsome young man, went to Paris in 1840 to study art, taking almost no instruction, but working in the Louvre and from models. He began as a Romanticist, seeing himself in early self-portraits as a rather Byronic figure. The Revolution of 1848 swept away the last vestiges of Courbet's romantic tendencies, and, a Socialist with an instinctive dislike of the new middle-class, he became a Realist, able to paint only what he saw: the world around him and the simple life of plain people. By 1849, such naturalistic works as *The Stone-Breakers* (destroyed 1945 in the bombing of Dresden) indicated by his choice of subject and treatment that he had answered Baudelaire's plea for paintings that expressed "the heroism of modern life." Courbet's own life was fairly heroic for he was both greatly admired and greatly detested as an artist. He was

also imprisoned for his part in the uprising of the Commune in 1871, spent six months in prison, left prison to live in exile in Switzerland and died there, still owing the French government a large sum charged to him for the destruction of the Vendôme column. Throughout his life he fought with both government authorities and public taste and continued to paint as he pleased, luckily, for as Ingres said of him in 1849, ". . . he is an eye." Courbet saw the world in which he was brought up; people; animals, wild and tame; fruits and flowers; fish; nudes; landscapes and seascapes. His palette, at first dark or restrained, grew warmer and brighter as he grew older. A master of pure technique, he could apply paint as smoothly as enamel or in thick corrugations; his ability to paint texture, particularly of animal pelts, was matchless; his fruits are round and full, bursting with sweetness; his flowers delicately differentiated. To inanimate objects, Courbet brought life; to human beings, love and understanding.

48

JEAN FRANÇOIS MILLET

French

1814-1875

THE GLEANERS

Musée du Louvre, Paris

Jean François Millet was born in Gréville, near Cherbourg. The artist who was to call himself the "peasant of peasants" spent his boyhood working in his father's fields. He studied first with a local painter in Cherbourg and then received a municipal grant that enabled him to go to Paris. There he studied with Paul Delaroche and at the Beaux-Arts, but the inflexible training was too much for his temperament. He gave up formal study to work alone in the Louvre and for years supported himself by painting portraits, pastorals, signboards, and decorative panels in the eighteenth-century manner. He was admitted to the French Academy in 1847. The following year, 1848, he exhibited *The Winnower,* his first painting of a peasant subject, and was accused of socialism by the critics. He retired to the village of Barbizon in 1849 to remain for twenty-two years, painting landscapes as well as scenes of rustic life with peasants and laborers. During the Franco-Prussian War Millet moved back to Cherbourg and painted some seascapes.

The French government commissioned him to do a set of decorative panels of *The Four Seasons* for the Pantheon. Millet made the preliminary sketches but died before he could begin the paintings. Millet and his Barbizon contemporaries painted the landscape in its natural state, thus breaking with the academic tradition that had immediately preceded them and of which David was the leader.

Millet's understanding and sympathy for the peasant in the fields and for his backbreaking labor are expressed sincerely and with great dignity. *The Gleaners* was attacked as expressing subversive political principles. It was revolutionary only in its effect upon art, for it is an honest portrayal of an everyday scene in the fields. The bent figures become one with the land over which they stoop in the golden peace of a late summer day. Faceless, they do not protest as they perform their work with a movement that has a cosmic rhythm in tune with nature, and so become a part of the ageless land.

49

NATHANIEL CURRIER and JAMES IVES

American

1813-1895 and 1824-1895

HOME TO THANKSGIVING

The Harry T. Peters Collection, Museum of the City of New York

The lithographic process of printing from a specially prepared stone was discovered by accident in Munich in 1796, and was introduced to the United States by Pendleton thirty years later. Nathaniel Currier was apprenticed to this first American lithographer at about the age of eighteen. Currier went into the printing business for himself in 1834 and a few years later saw the possibilities of using lithographed pictures for the news media. His first three important prints recorded fires, the third showing the 1840 fire on the steamboat *Lexington*. However, it was not until 1857, when Currier took James Ives as a partner, that the real flood of over 5,000 prints began and the coverage was extended to include news, sports, transportation, patriotic, juvenile, landscape, and genre subjects. Three new prints appeared each week until about 1875, when the appearance of illustrated magazines and news photos by daguerreotype put the partners out of business.

Currier and Ives prints were produced in two ways. Painters could make preliminary watercolor sketches which were then copied onto the stone by craftsmen, or artists could draw directly on the stone. Printing in the earliest Currier and Ives prints was in black and white, with color added by hand on each copy. Later, with the invention of chromolithography, large areas were printed in separate overprintings of each color, while only tiny details of color were applied by hand. This preservation of nineteenth-century everyday life and events was not only historically invaluable, but was also of great artistic merit. In addition, the low price to the public—twenty-five cents per print—brought art into the American home and greatly stimulated interest in painting and drawing.

50
THOMAS CHAMBERS
American
active 1834-1852
THE CONSTITUTION AND THE GUERRIERE
The Metropolitan Museum of Art, New York
Gift of Edgar William and Bernice Chrysler Garbisch, 1962

Thomas Chambers has been almost a complete mystery until quite recently. His place and date of birth have still not been discovered and the date of his death is equally unknown. We do know that he lived at various addresses in New York City between 1834 and 1841, listing himself on the city rolls first as a landscape artist and in 1838 as a marine artist. Between 1843 and 1852, he lived in Boston, where he called himself simply "artist." Where he lived between 1841 and 1843 is not known, but it is fairly reasonable to assume that he moved about the Hudson Valley since he painted Kingston, New York. About forty to fifty paintings of his have been discovered, the earliest one dated and signed 1835. Unlike other Chambers paintings attributed because of style or signature, this first painting, a marine copied from an engraving of the period, is painted on wood rather than on canvas. Chambers painted land-scapes, harbor views, and marine scenes, sometimes making original works and sometimes copying engravings. His work is distinctive for its brilliant, sunny color, his excellent draughtsmanship, his shining cloud formations, and for his rhythmical repetitions of large masses of cliffs and headlands. His careful, neat painting of figures, foliage, and small houses, as well as rock markings, mark him a primitive, but his works have a natural sweep that indicates greater than average ability and comprehension of the art of painting landscapes and seascapes. Among the places that he painted were New York Bay, Bedloes Island, Weehawken, Kingston, and other Hudson River spots, and among the engravings that he copied was Thomas Birch's famous *"United States and Macedonian,"* with a more accurate painting of the rigging of the ships indicating a knowledge greater than that of the subject's original painter.

51

HONORE DAUMIER
French
1808-1879

RODIN SUR LES BARRICADES
Narodni Galerie, Prague

Honoré Daumier was born in Marseilles. His family moved to Paris when he was quite young and, since his father found it difficult to provide for his wife and children, Honoré worked first as a bailiff's clerk and then as assistant in a bookshop. He had a great desire to draw, but the little art training he had soon bored him and he took to visiting the Louvre and walking about Paris studying faces. He learned the lithographic technique from a friend and, by the time he was twenty-one, had published cartoons in two newspapers. He continued this occupation for almost all of his life, except for a brief period (1860-64) when he had no work and would have starved if friends had not arranged for him to have a small government pension. From the time he was forty, however, Daumier's heart was in oil painting. Often he painted all day and worked all night to complete the lithographs which kept him alive. Daumier did not show his paintings while he was alive; only his closest friends knew they existed. Highly prized today, these paintings were sold by his widow for pennies, after Daumier, nearly blind from his long years of overwork, died of a stroke in 1879.

52

GEORGE CALEB BINGHAM

American

1811-1879

FUR TRADERS DESCENDING THE MISSOURI

The Metropolitan Museum of Art, New York, Morris K. Jesup Fund, 1933

George Caleb Bingham was born in the Piedmont country of Virginia where he remained until 1819 when a turn in fortune forced his family to move to Franklin, Missouri. In 1823, his father died and the Binghams moved to a farm outside the city, where the sons labored like grown men under the stern eye of Mrs. Bingham, from which Caleb escaped, whenever he could, to study the fascinating life on the Missouri River from a bluff near the farm. At sixteen, he was apprenticed to a cabinet-maker in Columbia, Missouri, an occupation that led inevitably to sign-painting. By the time he was 22, Caleb was travelling up and down the rivers painting portraits, in a strongly drawn and linear style, with strong color applied in large areas, a manner that he probably acquired from seeing ancestral portraits in the settlers' homes. His art was much appreciated locally as an indication of the progress of refinement beyond the Mississippi, but he received less acclaim when he opened a studio in St. Louis in 1835. Bingham realized that he must move from Missouri to be a better artist and after some study at the Pennsylvania Academy of Fine Art, he moved to Washington in 1840, again to paint portraits. Sitters were few and Bingham, always interested in politics, returned to Missouri in 1844 for the campaign of

Henry Clay versus James Polk. Bingham favored Clay but his painted banners did not win the election and, as a result, the artist began the series of genre pictures of river life that made him the historian of Jacksonian Democracy. In his river paintings, we see only male figures, never at work, but dancing, making music, playing cards, fishing, holding conversations, or sleeping, and never afflicted by the presence of women as they relax against generalized river backgrounds that recede mistily and glow smokily in the distance. His paintings present a composition based on the pyramid with its base parallel to the lower horizontal. His foreground figures stand quite free and are sharply delineated. He laid out his compositions carefully, drew his figures from life, realistically and often humorously, using friends for models and changing faces to suit his needs. In his crowded political canvasses, he grouped his figures in horizontal planes in alternating bands of light and shade. His work is fresh and vigorous, truthful and enthusiastic, and his finest works were painted between 1845 and 1855 when he painted the people and the country he loved, and before he went to Düsseldorf to exchange his arbitrary composition and lighting for the more sophisticated European style that weakened his natural strength.

53

REGIS GIGNOUX
American
1816-1882
WINTER SCENE
The Corcoran Gallery of Art, Washington, D.C.

Régis Gignoux was born in Lyons, France where he studied with Delaroche, the French painter of historical scenes and portraits. One of a constant stream of Europeans who have come to this country to paint the American scene and one of the earliest, Gignoux came to the United States in 1840 and began to paint landscapes, choosing for his specialties scenes of brilliant autumnal foliage and snow scenes. The latter were almost never handled by the Hudson River artists and Gignoux, a practical Frenchman, had enough training and familarity with the works of European landscapists to be able to paint actual winter landscapes without the necessity of plunging through drifts to get his effects. The works of Aart van der Neer had taught him how to paint snow and Hobbema's had taught him how to paint clouds. Gignoux's snow scenes are charming and have a faintly Euro-

pean tinge in their selection of views and buildings, while his works have a smooth thick quality deriving from his application of paint, whether oil or watercolor. By 1864, Gignoux was considered the best foreign painter to capture the American scene and by some critics as the equal of Church, Cole, and Durand. Certainly his works equalled theirs in popularity with the American people, for his *Niagara in Winter* was a serious contender to Church's famous painting of the falls in summer. Gignoux was also important in the formulation of George Inness, for, although Inness preferred to believe himself entirely self-taught, it was with Gignoux that he took lessons in 1844 and it was Gignoux's formulas that Inness modified for his early works. Gignoux returned to France in 1870 and continued his career with as much success as he had had in the United States.

54

SETH EASTMAN
American
1815-1875

LACROSSE PLAYING AMONG THE SIOUX
The Corcoran Gallery of Art, Washington, D.C.

Seth Eastman was born in Maine and graduated from West Point in 1829. He also taught drawing at the Academy from 1833 to 1840 between posts in the West where he had made sketches of the Indians as curiosities since he preferred to paint in the East, forgetting the harsh life among the "savages" by capturing Hudson River scenes. In 1841, he married a young lady who had literary aspirations and when Eastman was stationed at Fort Snelling she proceeded to write Indian romances (one of them is said to have inspired Longfellow's *Hiawatha*) for which her husband provided the illustrations drawing Sioux and Chippewas. He offered his original drawings "to any distinguished college" that would provide his children with a free education, and later used them to illustrate Schoolcraft's six volume text on the tribes. Eastman also used the drawings as the bases for oil paintings in the style of the Old Masters and with a thick oil technique. His sketches have the immediacy of factual recordings of Indian life and country. Eastman was one of several successors to George Catlin whose opinion of the nobility of the Indian he did not share, a point of view easily understood when we remember that Eastman, a professional officer, had the task of holding the Indians in check. He considered the braves as under the sway of "ungoverned passions" and the squaws as subjected to "superstition and degradation." *The American Aboriginal Portfolio,* published by Eastman and his wife Mary in Philadelphia in 1853, remains a valuable document, as does his *Sketchbook, 1848-1849*. Unfortunately, a great many of Eastman's finished oil paintings were destroyed in the Smithsonian Institute fire which took place in the late nineteenth century.

55

KOSON
Japanese
1801-1866

ON THE WING
Bibliotheque Nationale, Paris

Ikeda Sanshin, whose studio name was Koson, was born in Echigo. He went to Edo (Tokyo) at an early age and learned of the eighteenth-century artist Hoit-su. However, Koson began to study Chinese paintings of the Ming dynasty and subsequently changed his style. His work has something of the quality of the Chinese painter Lin Liang, famous for his paintings of game birds in their natural habitats. Koson has put music into his work. His masterpieces are few in number, but world-renowned.

On the Wing is a painting of ducks done in exquisitely sensitive coloring. The background is in tones of light blue. Across the panel, past the pale circle of the sun in the sky, fly the delicately detailed birds. The composition is airy and light with a graceful feeling of both depth and height.

56

WILLIAM SIDNEY MOUNT

American

1807-1868

THE LONG STORY

The Corcoran Gallery of Art, Washington, D.C.

William Sidney Mount, the first of the long line of *genre* painters to record the simple realities of American life, was born in Long Island, the son and grandson of tavern keepers of Setauket and Stony Brook. Two of his elder brothers were painters and he learned his profession in the sign-painting shop in New York City of one of them, Henry Smith Mount. William Mount's talent led to his being asked to work as an assistant to Henry Inman, the portraitist, but the young man's interests and tastes led him rapidly back to his family and in 1836 to Long Island and the atmosphere and people he knew and liked best. His greatest desire was to be completely original, "to avoid the style of any artist," and particularly European artists, and to create a naturalistic school of his own. An excellent draftsman, he combined this ability with careful composition, clarity of light, and the application of clear opaque pigment as craftsmen do, using the thickest paint for his foregrounds and the lightest for the sky. Since Long Island in that period offered a complete cross-section of eastern

American rural life, he painted scenes of courtship, music-making, dancing, playing games, fishing, and hunting. His works included a great many Negro figures whom he saw, by no means condescendingly, just as contentedly happy and busy or relaxed as were their white companions or masters. Mount's people live in an exceptionally idealistic world of neat barns and barnyards, freshly painted boats, picturesque but clean rags —in the neo-Classic tradition of what farm life should be. His paintings with their quiet humor and genuine delight in the subjects portrayed were extremely popular and were copied as lithographs by Currier and Ives for sale in the United States and by Goupil for European markets. The Civil War upset Mount considerably, he was a Copperhead who blamed the rift on the Abolitionists, and for the last few years of his life, he made only small *genre* sketches, as many as nine on a sheet of paper less than a foot square, but the desire to paint the finished pictures had gone, and he died, disillusioned, by the upheaval of the world around him.

57

JEAN-BAPTISTE CAMILLE COROT
French
1796-1875
BELFRY, AT DOUAI
Musée du Louvre, Paris

Jean-Baptiste Camille Corot was born in Paris, son of a wealthy cloth merchant. His father expected him to enter the family business and for a time Corot acceded to this wish, but eventually persuaded his father to let him pursue an artistic career. His father agreed and gave him a personal income, so that Corot never knew the hardships of many of his fellow artists. Although he began painting late in life, he was quickly established as a success and contributed many paintings to the Salon, to whose jury of admission he was elected in 1848. By 1855, after his exhibition at the Exposition Universelle when Napoleon III bought one of his works, Corot was in great demand. He continued to paint and travelled a great deal, making studies in Italy, southern France, and Switzerland for incorporation into larger works completed in Paris. Corot's work is a transition between early nineteenth-century Classicism and the later Romantic sensibility toward nature. Corot studied nature but did not copy it literally; he restricted his palette to misty greens and created a soft atmosphere by overpainting while his underpainting was still wet. Widely known for his generosity, he helped many artists and students in their careers, giving money freely and often signing the works of students to further their beginning careers. It is for this reason that the French say that Corot painted two thousand pictures of which three thousand are in American museums. Corot died in 1875 after a long and successful career. Corot is best known for his landscapes. However, he also painted a great many figure studies in order to experiment with various styles and methods.

58

THOMAS COLE

American

1801-1848

THE OXBOW (The Connecticut River near Northampton)

The Metropolitan Museum of Art, New York
Gift of Mrs. Russell Sage, 1908

Thomas Cole, the leading figure of the Hudson River school, was born in Lancashire, England, where he was a textile designer and engraver. He came to America in 1818, and taught drawing and painting, studied wood engraving, and was an itinerant portrait painter before entering The Pennsylvania Academy of Fine Arts in 1823, where he was much impressed by the landscapes of Birch and Doughty. He moved to New York City in 1825 and after a summer roaming the Catskills made a successful debut as a landscapist. Cole's expression of God in nature and the primeval aspect of the American scene was romantically displayed in his thunderous landscapes, strongly contrasted in light and shade, and dramatically composed. His work was enthusiastically accepted and when he decided to go to Europe for further study, the opinion of his friends was best summed up by the closing line of William Cullen Bryant's sonnet addressed to Cole: "But keep that earlier, wilder image bright." During his 1829-1832 visit, he went to England, France, and Italy,

discovering Turner, Claude, and Raphael. He did not, however, abandon his particularly American way of painting or looking at nature and for the rest of his life straddled the depth between the more conservative Europeans and "the wilder image," painting not only landscapes but enormous allegories: *The Course of Empire* (1836) and *The Voyage of Life* (1839). Cole, already ill, returned to Italy in 1841, shutting himself away in a studio in Rome, to paint a second version of *The Voyage of Life*. This was poorly received in Rome and Cole returned to the Catskills in 1842, where, as his health grew steadily worse, his only comforts were his family and his beloved mountains. Depressed and tormented, he spent the remainder of his short life painting the romantic, realistic landscapes that were his finest expressions. Cole's contribution to the development of painting in America was enormous; he literally founded the Native School of landscape painting, keeping a firm grasp on earlier tradition and reaching out for what was to come, always remaining inherently American.

59

THEODORE GERICAULT
French
1791-1842

OFFICER OF THE IMPERIAL GUARD ON HORSEBACK
Musée du Louvre, Paris

Jean Louis André Théodore Géricault was born in Rouen. He studied in Paris with Carle Vernet and with Guérin. His earliest works were sculptural drawings in the manner of Michelangelo and it came as a considerable surprise when he offered to the 1812 Salon a Baroque painting entitled *Officer of the Imperial Guard,* a striking painting of the officer on a plunging horse in a smoky, cloudy atmosphere of flame and fire. Horses were Géricault's passion and one was to cause his death. He continued to paint battle scenes and in his enthusiasm joined the Bourbon Musketeers and fought as a cavalry officer for the Restoration of the French royal house. Géricault went to Italy in 1816 and remained for three years, copying old masters and classical art. When he returned to France he painted *The Raft of the Medusa,* thus associating himself with humanitarian causes. The painting was not well received by the French government and Géricault took it to England on a triumphant tour. The influence of English art upon Géricault's style showed in an abandonment of his extremely dramatic style for a more down-to-earth one. Upon his return to Paris, Géricault was commissioned by a doctor of the Salpétrière Hospital to do facial studies of the insane. In 1824, as the result of a fall from a horse, Géricault died at the age of thirty-two; his career had spanned only fifteen years. His works show a powerful, energetic temper, a Romanticism thoroughly in keeping with his youth and the age in which he lived, and a germ of the Realism that was to follow. This combination made him extremely influential upon the generation of artists to come.

60

EUGENE DELACROIX
French
1798-1863

HORSE FRIGHTENED BY STORM
Hungarian National Gallery, Budapest

Eugene Delacroix, the greatest of the French Romantic painters, was born near Paris. He began his studies in Bordeaux and seemed at first destined for a musical career, but went to Paris in 1805 to attend the Lycée Louis-le-Grand where he received a standard classical education and had as a classmate, Géricault. Delacroix was then encouraged by an uncle to whom he showed some sketches to study art with Guérin and then to go on to the Beaux-Arts. There, he was soon dissatisfied with the academic training but was encouraged by the early success of Géricault, now his friend and fellow-student. Delacroix's early interests in art included the English landscapists and portraitists and Hogarth. His debut at the 1821 Salon with *Dante and Virgil,* a romantic and frightening work, was crowned by the purchase of the painting by the French government. In 1824, *The Massacre at Scio,* called by critics a "massacre of painting", established Delacroix as one of those intellectuals who believed that the world could be made better and as one on the side of struggling, unhappy people everywhere. A visit to England and to English artists in 1825 was followed by other romantic paintings and his first period ended in 1830 with *Liberty Leading the People,* a work glorifying revolt and heart-rending in its portrayal of the dead and dying. With this he became the head of the Romantic School, but the failure of the Revolution of 1830 made it necessary for him to express himself in literary and exotic paintings such as those resulting from a trip to Morocco in 1832. Delacroix also painted animals, portraits of musicians, religious subjects, and great original murals, indicative of his love for the works of the Renaissance. Delacroix's works are gloriously exciting; even the most calm seem bursting with awareness of life; his portraits burn with an inner fire. With marvelously fluid brushwork and a rich glowing palette, deep reds, blues, and greens, creamy whites, golden flesh-tones, he created a world removed from drab reality, theatrical perhaps, but none the less ecstatic. Delacroix, who had had bouts of fever as early as 1820, died in 1863, still sketching and making entries in the Journal he had kept for years.

61

THOMAS SULLY

American

1783-1872

THE TORN HAT

Thomas Sully was born in England to a family of actors and was brought to Charleston, South Carolina, as a child. His first artistic training came from his brother-in-law, a French émigré miniaturist named Belfons. He then worked with his own brother, Lawrence Sully, also a miniaturist. Although very poor, Sully was intent on improving his technique and studied the works of such artists as Bembridge and Gilbert Stuart. After attaining American citizenship in 1809, he managed to go to England to study with King and Benjamin West, financed by his own savings and by funds from generous patrons who paid him in advance to make copies of the old masters. After a year in England, he returned to Philadelphia to paint portraits. He was extremely successful—so much so, in fact, that he was commissioned by the St. George Society to paint his most famous portrait, that of Queen Victoria. Sully lived to a ripe old age, honored and successful in his chosen career.

Boy with a Torn Hat is a brilliantly lit, skillfully painted example of Sully's style which, in its polish and assurance, is rather like that of the English portraitist Sir Thomas Lawrence. The color is fresh and clear, and the contrast between the dark background and the boy's high color makes him appear young and innocent. The drawing is accomplished and the paint easily applied so that the entire composition is appealing and handsome. The boy seems unaware of his good looks and is, if we may judge by the torn straw hat, more interested in going fishing than in sitting for his portrait.

62

THOMAS BIRCH

American

1779-1851

VIEW OF THE DELAWARE NEAR PHILADELPHIA

The Corcoran Gallery of Art, Washington, D.C.

Thomas Birch was born in London and came to live in Philadelphia in 1794 with his father, William Birch, an engraver and miniature painter. The elder Birch trained his son to follow in his footsteps and between 1798 and 1800, father, son, and another artist made a famous set of engravings *View of Philadelphia* in the very popular topographical style. In such works, the object is the exact rendering of as many natural objects as possible, those in the background of a landscape being larger in size, but all of the objects are equally carefully rendered and colored according to nature (blue skies, green trees, etc.) in even washes without gradations for distance or changes in light. At about this time also, Thomas Birch painted one topographical oil, *Penn's Treaty Tree,* a work often reproduced and very well-known. This simple style of vernacular art did not long interest Thomas Birch, for a visit in 1807 to the Delaware Capes awoke in him a love for the sea. Although he probably studied Vernet's French sea port studies from engravings, his own seascapes are much simpler in manner and more closely allied to the works of 17th century Dutch artists. The War of 1812 led to his composition of a series of oils representing famous battleships and sea battles. Of these, *The "United States" and the "Macedonian,"* is the finest and shows Birch's qualities at their best. The ships strain at their sails and are alive on moving water, the air is light and fresh, and a gently romantic atmosphere pervades the scene. For the next forty years, with an occasional variant landscape or snow scene, Birch painted the harbor views and marine scenes for which he is best known. His works together with those of Thomas Doughty, who was his slightly younger contemporary, inspired Thomas Cole, the first great Romantic landscape painter.

63

EDWARD HICKS

American

1780-1849

THE PEACEABLE KINGDOM

Collection of Edgar William and Bernice Chrysler Garbisch

Edward Hicks was born in Attleboro, Pennsylvania. The son of a farmer, he left the land to become an apprentice to a coachmaker. He showed ability in painting coaches and signs but, becoming obsessed with a feeling of sin for having attended local farm festivals, he became a Quaker, gave up his brushes, and bought a farm. His farm did not prosper and he turned to itinerant preaching in the northern part of the United States and southern Canada. He earned great renown as a preacher but, in 1819, decided that a good Christian must earn his living with his hands. Since his only manual skill was painting, he went back to art and put on canvas his sincere beliefs in religion and peaceful cooperation. Hicks was entirely self-taught, since he believed that organized education was a tool of the devil. Ironically, with his paintings he himself has taught succeeding generations.

Hicks painted about twenty-five versions of *The Peaceable Kingdom,* an allegory of the American dream. In these paintings not only does the lion lie down with the lamb, but also the red man and white man stand companionably together and children frolic in a land of peace, plenty, and universal harmony. This is not simply milk-and-water sweetness, however, but rather a concept which understands that the lion and tiger must repress their stronger desires in order that peace be attained. Hicks' flesh-eating beasts are glaring-eyed and tense, in sharp contrast to the placid domestic animals, while the innocent children are as unaware of these tensions as the viewer is conscious of them. Hicks' message is as valid today as it was in 1819.

64
JOSEPH M. W. TURNER
English
1775-1851
SNOW STORM

Reproduced by courtesy of the Trustees,
The National Gallery, London

Joseph M. W. Turner, who was born in London, showed precocious talent as a child. He earned money coloring prints for an engraver when he was in his early teens, took drawing lessons, copied in Reynolds' studio, and was admitted to the Royal Academy Schools, exhibiting at the Royal Academy by the time he was fifteen. He had his own studio at the age of eighteen, and before he was twenty his drawings were being reproduced as prints. He was made an Associate of the Academy in 1799. Turner worked in watercolor and oils, painting landscapes and marine scenes. Turner became successively a full member of the Academy and its Professor of Perspective when he was only thirty-two. His success was, it would seem, com-plete, but Turner continued to progress, travel-ling abroad and studying the works of other mas-ters. The last phase of his career was his greatest, and his work was appreciated only by Ruskin; members of the Academy and other critics could not understand it. Turner's canvases now became moving symbols of natural forces, fire, smoke, rain, rapid movement of train and boats, the smother-ing of fog. These were the Turner paintings that impressed Monet on his visit to London in 1870 and cleared the way for the development of French Impressionism and, in fact, for all open-air paint-ing in the nineteenth century, as well as for the modern concepts behind natural phenomena and of a personal approach to any experience.

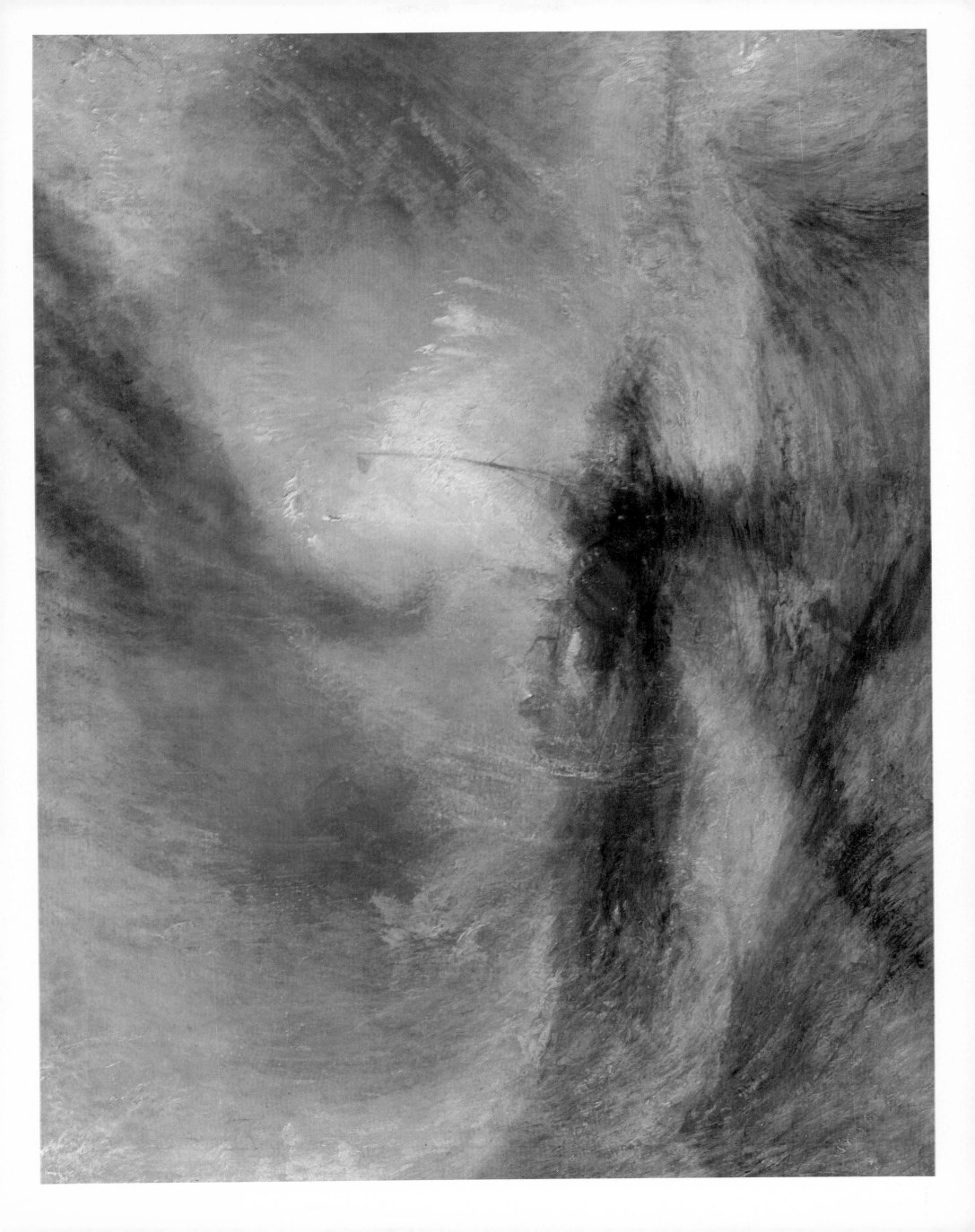

65

JOHN CONSTABLE

English

1776-1837

WEYMOUTH BAY

Reproduced by courtesy of the Trustees,
The National Gallery, London

John Constable was the son of a miller in Suffolk. Introduced to the work of Claude Lorrain by Sir George Beaumont, he painted in watercolor and sketched by himself until he was twenty-four, when he entered the Royal Academy School in London. Two years later he had his first exhibition, which passed almost unnoticed, for Constable, a forerunner of the Impressionists, painted in watercolor directly from nature and was the first to treat landscapes with spontaneity and emotion. The demand in England was for portraits, and Constable, to earn a meager living, painted portraits for which he cared nothing and painted landscapes for himself. When he was forty-eight, he sent several landscapes to the Paris Salon. The French were highly impressed and awarded him the Gold Medal (1824) for *Hay Wain*. Five years later Constable was finally elected to full membership in the Royal Academy. He considered that this honor had come too late. Constable's last years were lonely and embittered ones, for complete recognition of his talents and his technique of using broken touches of color to convey movement and light did not come until after his death.

66

JAMES PEALE

American

1749-1831

FRUIT

The Corcoran Gallery of Art, Washington, D.C.

James Peale, the youngest brother of the well-known painter Charles Willson Peale, was born in Chestertown, Maryland. As a young man, he learned and practiced the trades of saddlery, carpentry, and cabinet-making for he did not decide to become a painter until 1770. He then took lessons from his brother, who had studied with Benjamin West in London, in watercolor and oil painting. James Peale, a Captain in the Revolutionary Continental Army, resigned his commission in 1779 and returned to his brother's home in Philadelphia. The careers of the two brothers were closely linked and James assisted Charles not only in painting but with the natural history museum that the elder had founded and in which he used paintings as backgrounds for objects displayed. One result of this museum was that Charles Willson Peale taught his brother, his own son Raphaelle, and James' four daughters to paint still lifes in the style known as the Peale manner. The composition was shallow and limited and most typically consisted of a life-like and careful arrangement of fruit in a bowl placed on a table whose top was cut in sharply at a right angle, thus bringing up the rear wall as background. The straight lines of the table top and the canvas were contrasted to and cut by the natural oval or circular shapes of the fruits, whose rounded forms protruded gently outward. In October of 1786, the brothers decided to divide up their painting business, James becoming the specialist in miniatures. He did not limit himself, however, and also painted landscapes, historical subjects, and small portraits, eventually developing an individual style that is distinguished by precise and delicate draughtsmanship, light tonalities, and a light palette in portraits. In 1818, James Peale's eyesight failed and he began to specialize in the still lifes in the decorative and botanical method described, changing his palette for a more sombre one for the backgrounds. The canvases were usually small, strong in composition, and appealing because of the care and pleasure with which they presented ordinary objects in a surface that was absolutely flat in application of paint but effectively brightened with shadows and highlights.

67

GILBERT STUART

American

1755-1828

GEORGE WASHINGTON

The Corcoran Gallery of Art, Washington, D.C.

Gilbert Stuart was born in Newport, Rhode Island, the son of an insignificant snuff-grinder. As a boy, Stuart was fairly wild and given to boyish pranks, but he was already painting on commission by the time he was fourteen. Prominent citizens of Newport sent him to study with Cosmo Alexander, a visiting Scottish portraitist, who took the gifted Stuart back to Edinburgh with him in 1770. Two years later, Alexander died and Stuart worked his way home on a sailing ship to set up as a portraitist in a manner that proved that he had not absorbed the elegant techniques of 18th century British and Scotch artists. When the American Revolution broke out, Stuart left for London where, upon discovering that his rough American style did not please the English, he studied with Benjamin West, learning from him how to paint the gleam of satin and silk and the translucence of flesh. When Stuart opened his own studio, he was phenomenally and very rapidly successful, for West's training had opened the path to his own natural genius. Stuart, however, was an excessively nervous man and he began to drink heavily to quiet his nerves. His excesses led to debt and to avoid debtor's prison, he fled from Great Britain and returned to the United States in the winter of 1782-1783. Once in his own country and freed from the necessity of competition with the English artists, Stuart who once said that "flesh is like no other substance under heaven" could paint portraits as he saw fit, almost totally eliminating backgrounds and bodies to concentrate on physiognomy and character, achieving his effects by his brilliant treatment of skin tones. The Vaughan portrait of George Washington tells us, at once, that Washington exemplified the necessary qualities for leadership; he has no need for symbols or decoration to indicate either his rank or his greatness. That this portrait still symbolizes the underlying principles of the Constitution and the Bill of Rights is proof enough that Stuart had translated into art the ideals of the founding fathers; he had transmuted what he learned in Europe into something uniquely American.

68

JEAN HONORE FRAGONARD
French
1732-1806
LE BILLET DOUX
The Metropolitan Museum of Art, New York
The Jules S. Bache Collection, 1949

Jean Honoré Fragonard was born in Provence in the town of Grasse which he left at the age of eighteen for Paris where he studied with Boucher and possibly with Chardin. After obtaining the Prix de Rome in 1752, he studied with Carle Van Loo and Lépicié before going to Rome in 1756. In 1759, Fragonard and his contemporary Hubert Robert were invited on a trip to southern Italy and Sicily by the Abbé de Saint-Non. The two young men, each strongly influencing the other, sketched and painted archaeological scenes, landscapes, and religious and *genre* works, small in size. Fragonard during the trip had the opportunity to study the richly colored and highly lit works of the Neapolitan painters and, returning to Paris in 1761, by way of Venice, also studied his Venetian contemporaries and the works of older masters, Venetian, Dutch, and Flemish, some of whose works he copied. Upon his return to France, Fragonard was admitted to the Academy with a work more classical in subject than in execution and then, in 1765, gave up historical and religious paintings to work in the style for which he is best known, landscapes and interiors peopled with enchanting young lovers, cupids, Venuses, in a refreshing light atmosphere of pure joy in living. Among his most

famous patrons were Madame de Pompadour, the financier Bergeret (who accompanied him to Italy again in 1773) and Madame du Barry for whom he painted the great panels of *Progress in Love,* now in the Frick Museum in New York. Du Barry refused the completed works and Fragonard kept them in his own home, taking them with him to Grasse when he fled the Terror in 1790. The artist returned to Paris, where he had already received official recognition, and was made a member of the Jury of Arts and received a post in the newly created Louvre Museum. He had, however, outlived his period and the sober thought of the Revolutionary period, led in painting by David, could not include Fragonard, who, ousted from his Louvre apartment in 1806, and deprived of his pension, died in the same year, reduced to poverty.

One of the most brilliantly original French painters of the late 18th century, Fragonard painted with a spontaneity and a fluidity of technique that recall Rubens. His imagination, delicate wit, and refinement combined to create volatile poetic canvases that present the best aspects of the period of Louis XVI with skilled, piercing observation just as Watteau had presented the Regency period some fifty years before.

69

JOSHUA REYNOLDS
English
1723-1792

MASTER HARE
Musée du Louvre, Paris

Sir Joshua Reynolds was born in Devonshire, the son of a Fellow of Balliol College, Oxford. His father apprenticed him to a portrait painter, and by the time he was twenty Reynolds was painting portraits in Plymouth Dock. Reynolds spent the years 1749 to 1752 in Italy, studying the Italian masters and earning a living by painting portraits of English visitors. Reynolds returned to London via Paris and settled there, where his success was soon remarkable. Reynolds was extremely ambitious personally and sought social advancement by currying the favor of his noble and wealthy sitters. He was eminently successful in his advancement, and when the Royal Academy was founded in 1768 he became its first president and was knighted by George III. The collection of his speeches given at the Academy's annual banquet, published as *Discourses,* is an important statement of eighteenth-century artistic principles, which included the raising of the status of the artist, the importance of authority, and a striving for dignity and taste. Reynolds' portraits have great dignity and grace and are in themselves a history of the life of the upper classes in eighteenth-century England. They are painted with assurance and a basic psychological comprehension of the sitters that goes beyond the surface effect.

The charming little boy in *Master Hare* is full of mischief, and in spite of what we might consider today a girlish haircut and clothing, he is all boy. The face is masculine. Such a portrait with its unposed stance and mischievous expression was quite revolutionary in Reynolds' time, when children were supposed to be seen and not heard and to be portrayed as little dolls or smaller images of their parents. Master Hare, for all his gentle breeding, is presented in a very unconventional way. He is a child who will grow up to be a man.

70
FRANCISCO GOYA
Spanish
1746-1828
THE MAJA CLOTHED
Museo Nacional del Prado, Madrid

Francisco Goya, one of the greatest and most original of Spanish painters, was born in Fuendetodos and took his first art lessons from his father, a master gilder. Goya learned the art of etching from the monks in Saragossa and began his career in Madrid in the tradition of the Spanish official art of his time: a compendium of borrowings from Italian Baroque, French Rococo, and Neo-Classicism. Twice rejected as a student by the Madrid Academy of Fine Arts, Goya went to Italy in 1766 and returned in 1771 to paint frescoes in Saragossa in a Rococo manner. He then became a court painter in 1786 at the courts of Carlos III and IV, and painted a series of brilliant court portraits. In 1792 he fell ill and lost his hearing, and, during his convalescence, the great Goya—introverted, sarcastic, humanistic, expressionistic—emerged, peeping through the silvery *Caprichos* to indulge in biting satire on social mores with more than a hint of double meanings. His last great public comission was for the church of San Antonio de la Florida, in Madrid, in 1798. The Napoleonic invasion of 1808, with its horrible and cruel killings, and the death of the Duchess of Alba completed the transfiguration of Goya. His etch-

ings from then on were as acid as the material used on the plates and his paintings became Romantic and Expressionistic. In 1814 Goya, disliking the rule of Ferdinand VII, retired to a house in the country and adorned his walls with the so-called "Black" frescoes—pessimistic, imaginative images of humanity, degraded and bestial, terrible, fascinating, and hallucinatory to see. At the fall of the *Cortes* in 1824, Goya retreated to voluntary exile in Bordeaux, where he died in 1828.

Legend has it that *The Maja Clothed (Maja Dressed)* was posed for by the Duchess of Alba, but this now seems highly improbable, since the technique is that of a later period, after the death of the Duchess. The work is quite Impressionistic, both in the color used for modeling in the dress, plastered to the figure as if it had been dipped in water, and in the careless pose of the feet with one slipper pointing directly at the viewer. The head is posed at a reckless angle and brushed in almost carelessly. The painting is sensuous in feeling and extremely delicate in tone, with a background of pale greens, paler violets, and pinks contrasting with golden flesh tones and a quite pink face.

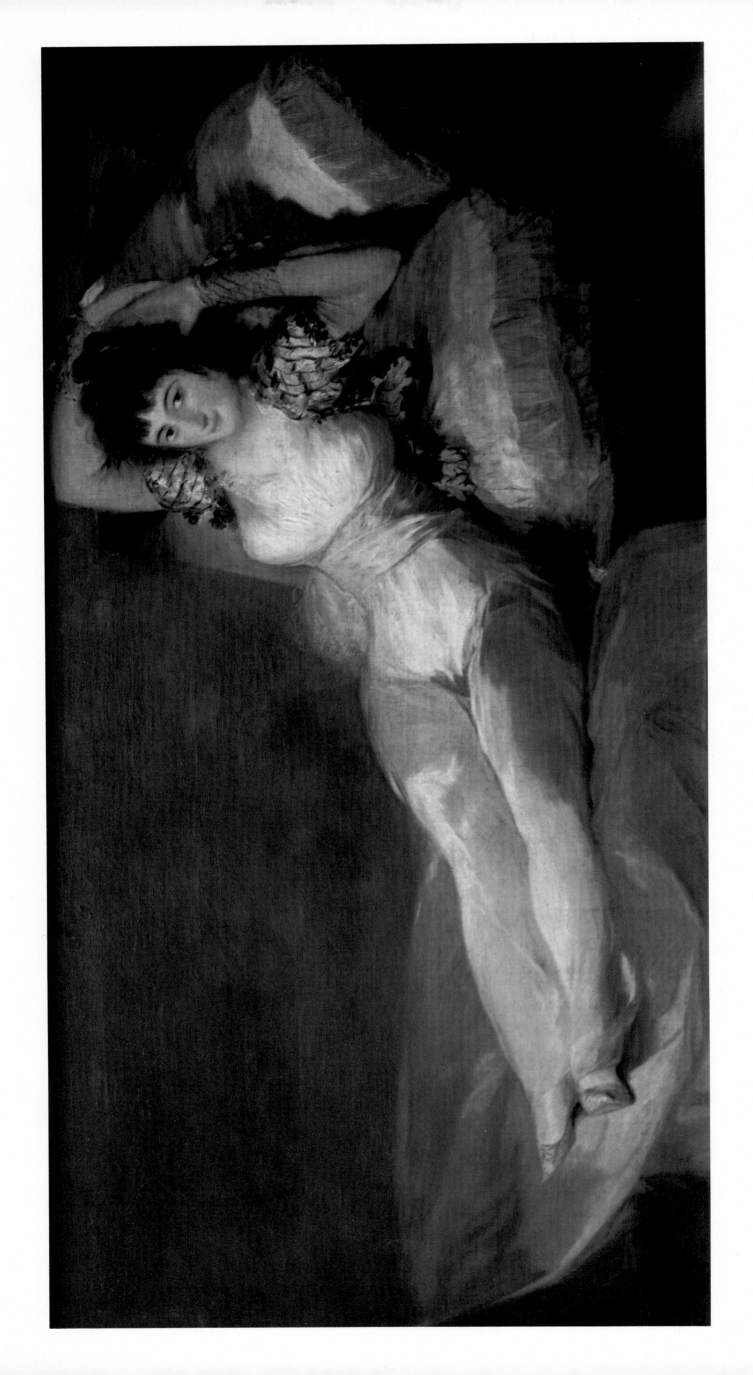

71

THOMAS GAINSBOROUGH
English
1727-1788
BLUE BOY
Henry E. Huntington Library and Art Gallery, San Marino

Thomas Gainsborough was born in Sudbury, Suffolk. His parents sent him to London when he was fourteen and he spent five years studying art with Hayman, an English designer and portraitist, and with Gravelot, a French illustrator and engraver. Gainsborough married an heiress when he was nineteen and the couple lived first in Ipswich and then in Bath. Gainsborough painted portraits of the landed gentry and nobility to earn money, and landscapes because he enjoyed doing them. Painting in the great houses enabled Gainsborough to see the works of such masters as Rubens, Van Dyck, and Watteau, all of whom influenced his work. Gainsborough moved to London in 1774, set up a studio, and soon rivaled Sir Joshua Reynolds in popularity. Gainsborough's skill in handling fabrics, the graceful charm of his works, and his use of harmonious color make him not only one of the long line of portrait painters who preceded him but also a forerunner of Renoir, while his landscapes link him to Watteau. A founding member of the Royal Academy in 1768, Gainsborough broke with that group in a quarrel over the hanging of his pictures in 1783. Upon his deathbed, he was reconciled to Sir Joshua Reynolds, with whom he had had serious differences.

72

WILLIAM HOGARTH
English
1697-1764

THE SHRIMP GIRL

Reproduced by courtesy of the Trustees,
The National Gallery, London

William Hogarth, the first painter to be a social critic, was born in London and as an apprentice learned the art of engraving on copper, book illustration, and the making of book plates and show cards. When he gained his independence in 1720, he began the study of painting with Sir James Thornhill, a painter of baroque decorations. Hogarth began his own career as a portraitist after his marriage to Thornhill's daughter, but it was not until the 1730's that he found the field suited to his own temperament and interests. He described his own works as "moral subjects . . . similar to representations on the stage" and wished them to be considered and judged as if they were dumb-shows. In 1731, the first six paintings called *The Harlot's Progress* appeared, and the following year Hogarth engraved the series for a large and enthusiastic popular audience. Other series followed: *The Rake's Progress, Marriage à la Mode, The Four Times of Day,* as well as single works depicting the life of his period. All of these teach by example and point out the foibles of the rich and the depths of degradation of those who have fallen from the narrow path of middle-class virtue. The paintings are crowded with a fascinating gallery of psychological and physical caricatures and portraits and illustrate satirically in paint the world depicted by such moralizing novelists as Henry Fielding and Samuel Richardson. The individual paintings are crammed with detail and allusions to each other, so that the viewer has the sensation of reading a story without words but with familiar characters, objects, and settings. The works are as bright and lively as some of the works of Watteau and as evidently delighted with human nature as are those of Frans Hals or Jan Steen. The moralizing, although clear, is never obtrusive or depressing, and these series are extremely important historical and social documents. Hogarth was less successful with his purely historical paintings and his sincere and powerful portraits, in which, nevertheless, his keen understanding of human nature and his ability to paint both boldly and minutely are more than evident.

73

JACOB ISAACKSZ van RUISDAEL
Dutch
1629-1682
COUP DE SOLEIL (Sunlight)
Musée du Louvre, Paris

Jacob van Ruisdael was born in Haarlem, where his father was a minor painter and frame-maker and his uncle, Salomon van Ruysdael, a well-known landscapist, gave him his first lessons in art. Ruisdael's earliest works, for the most part scenes of dunes and the adjoining coastal waters, show the influence of his uncle and of Cornelis Vroom and Jan van Goyen. The lovely country around Haarlem, a trip to the eastern part of Holland, and his acceptance of his contemporary Spinoza's pantheistic philosophy of nature combined to make Ruisdael the most emotional and poetic landscapist of the 17th century. In about 1655, Ruisdael moved to Amsterdam, became a citizen of that city and was listed on their rolls as a physician and an artist. Here he met and taught Hobbema and collaborated with such artists as Adriaen van Ostade, Berchem, and Van der Helst who supplied the occasional small figures in his landscapes. Each of these is an emotional expression of Ruisdael's own sensibility, a natural melancholy, and a feeling of the instability and evanescence of even those things that seem most enduring in nature itself. A Romantic before the era of Romanticism, Ruisdael painted both real and imaginary landscapes, castles, Gothic ruins, dark woodlands, tumbling, tempestuous waterfalls and rushing brooks. He invariably chose the most dramatic or mysterious moments to catch his realistic scenes: the time of twilight with its deepening shadows, sun bursting through clouds, or silvery moonlight, thus achieving strong contrasts of light and shade. His palette was quiet and subdued; his composition always unified and balanced with detail submerged into the larger view, thus creating effects that are expressions of mood, often solitary and brooding, sometimes ironic, but always lyrically poetic. Ruisdael remained in Amsterdam for nearly thirty years returning to Haarlem, ill and miserably poor, to die as quietly as he had lived.

74

FRANCESCO GUARDI

Italian

1712-1793

THE DOGE'S PALACE, VENICE

Reproduced by courtesy of the Trustees,
The National Gallery, London

Francesco Guardi was born in Venice. The son of a decorative painter, he studied first with his brother, a painter of Rococo altarpieces. Guardi later worked in Canaletto's workshop, taking from him some topographical influences. Guardi, however, was much more influenced by the works of Longhi, Ricci, and Magnasco; from the latter he inherited a taste for fantasy. Very little is known about his life, perhaps because he was so little regarded by his contemporaries, for his interest was not in architectural detail, but in reflection of light upon water and air. In his last works the subject became light, air, and water, and architecture almost disappeared from his land and seascapes. Guardi's works were painted almost entirely after 1760. He died in 1793.

Guardi painted Venetian scenes, marines, landscapes and portraits. *Doge's Palace* with Campanile Bell Tower illustrates his pre-occupation with the refraction of light from buildings, people and water. Architectural details are quite clearly defined but a general haziness is noticeable.

75

MEINDERT HOBBEMA

Dutch

1638-1709

THE RUINS OF BREDERODE CASTLE

Reproduced by courtesy of the Trustees,
The National Gallery, London

Meindert Hobbema was born in Amsterdam and never left that city except for brief sketching trips in its surrounding countryside. Hobbema, both pupil and friend of Ruisdael while that master lived in Amsterdam, specialized in landscape painting during a short career that ended abruptly in 1689, when, the year after his marriage to the Burgomaster's cook, he painted his last picture. The good offices of the Burgomaster secured him a civil service position as "wijnroeir" or minor customs official whose endless duty it was to gauge the amount of wine in foreign casks according to Dutch measure. Although this position assured him a steady salary and was more lucrative than the sale of paintings, Hobbema died a pauper in 1709, leaving behind work that ranks him with Ruisdael as extremely important in the history of art as one of the greatest of the 17th century Dutch landscape artists. Hobbema's paintings may be distinguished from those of Ruisdael by their placid-

ity, truthfulness, attention to small detail, and lack of passion. His skies, always so important in Holland where the sky is as important as the land for its palpable substance, its color, and its movement, are by no means cloudless, but they are never turbulent. His waters are harnessed or still and his trees, lovingly portrayed, seem not to move, even as they stretch upward to join earth and sky, breaking the monotony and making small enclosures that reveal man's need for intimacy. Hobbema's color is quietly soft, deep greens, the occasional red of a tiled roof, warm yellows, and the occasional flash of a white coif or collar, under the blue and white of the endless sky. His compositions are subtly balanced, adding to the serenity of his effects, and the detail of tree branches, country roads, small figures going about their daily tasks, adds to the feeling of serenity that in Hobbema seems to indicate that man may be content merely to be alive; to be as one with his environment.

76

JEAN-BAPTISTE SIMEON CHARDIN
French
1699-1779

UTENSILES DE CUISINE
Musée du Louvre, Paris

Jean Baptiste Siméon Chardin was born in Paris, the son of a master cabinetmaker. His artistic beginnings were modest and he began as a student of Pierre-Jacques Cazes, aided J. B. Van Loo in restorations of paintings at Fontainebleau, and painted a rifle on a canvas by Coypel. He attracted attention to himself by his painting of a surgeon's sign, which he decorated with a lively street scene instead of the usual symbols. He then began to paint still lifes that were very well received and went on from these to a series of *singeries* (paintings of monkeys dressed as humans and engaged in human activities) and to *genre* pictures of middle-class life. His paintings sold well, although cheaply, and were frequently published as engravings. Chardin became a member of the Royal Academy in 1728, one of its Counselors in 1743, and was Treasurer in 1755, putting its books in order and making businesslike reforms. His eyesight began to fail as he grew older and he turned to pastels before his death at the age of eighty. Chardin's work is a sharp break with tradition for he believed that anything was worth being painted. He chose simple objects and simple scenes, which he treated in a style notable for its homogeneous brushwork, skillful arrangement, use of light and shade, and a sobriety that is extremely appealing and has rarely been equalled.

77

JUDITH LEYSTER

Dutch

1609-c. 1660

THE JESTER

Rijksmuseum, Amsterdam

Judith Leyster was born in Haarlem. She was one of the rare women painters of her period and signed her works with her maiden name. Miss Leyster first became known as a painter in 1628 and became a member of the Haarlem Guild in 1633. Before this period, she lived for a while near Utrecht and came under the influence of Terbrugghen, a painter of religious pictures and a follower of Caravaggio. When she came to Haarlem, Miss Leyster became the pupil of Frans Hals. In 1635 she herself taught Willem Wouters. She married Jan Miense Molenaer, whose work also shows the influence of Hals, and it is possible that they were students together. Very highly regarded by her contemporaries, Miss Leyster painted so much like Frans Hals that many of her works were at first attributed to him.

The Jester, painted in warm reds, browns, and black, has indeed the unposed and impish quality of a Frans Hals and shows the same insight into character. Some notable differences are quite apparent, however. The lighting is less bold and comes from outside the canvas rather than from within it. One hand is in deep shadow and is more Impressionistically drawn. The entire work, moreover, is less bold. It is not feminine or sentimental, but it is less roistering in both pose and approach than Hals' *Boy with a Lute,* with which it should be compared. Neither picture detracts from the other—proof enough of the talent of both artists, and the world is grateful for both.

78

JEAN ANTOINE WATTEAU
French
1684-1721
THE EMBARKATION FOR CYTHERA
Musée du Louvre, Paris

Jean Antoine Watteau was born in Valenciennes when it had been French only six years. He is the epitome of witty, gay French art and is the recognized founder of the eighteenth-century Rococo art that broke away from the rather stuffy formalism of the classical art of Louis XIV's period. It has been argued that he takes his inspiration from Rubens, but Watteau's art, although also glorifying women, is much more delicate and graceful in imagery. Watteau arrived in Paris in 1702, after some study in Valenciennes. Poor and unknown, he nearly starved until he was taken in by Claude Audran, painter and Curator of the Luxembourg Palace. The paintings in the palace and its park and gardens influenced Watteau as strongly as had the scenic design for the Italian *Commedia dell' Arte* upon which he had worked with Gillot. Un-

successful in his attempt for the *Prix de Rome* in 1709, Watteau accepted the patronage of the financier Crozat, in whose house filled with Venetian and Flemish paintings and drawings he lived and worked until about 1717. Watteau's reputation in a small but important circle of people of taste was now assured. In 1712 he was nominated for the Academy in a new category, *Fêtes Galantes,* and was accepted in 1717 with *The Embarkation for Cythera* (Louvre version), an imaginative and lyrically poetic work depicting beautifully dressed ladies and gentlemen, in a magnificent landscape setting, bound for an unknown and romantic destination. In 1720 Watteau left Crozat's home and, desperately ill, went to England to consult Queen Anne's physician. His case was hopeless and he died of tuberculosis at the age of thirty-seven.

79

BARTOLOME ESTEBAN MURILLO

Spanish

1617-1682

THE YOUNG BEGGAR

Musée du Louvre, Paris

Bartolomé Esteban Murillo, often called the Spanish Raphael, was born in Seville and orphaned at the age of ten. An uncle placed him in the workshop of Juan del Castillo in Seville, and he began the career that led to his becoming the outstanding Spanish Baroque painter learning decoration. Murillo learned everything he knew about European and Spanish Art in Seville and during a three-year period in Madrid, where he saw collections of paintings that included works by Rubens, Correggio, and Raphael, Flemish and Italian engravings, as well as works by Velasquez and Ribera. Murillo's first important commission, 1645, was for the Franciscan Convent in Seville. The series, that told the history of the Franciscan Order, gained him great popularity. He was able to marry in 1648 and by 1654 was considered the finest painter of Seville, ran a crowded workshop, and received constant commissions for sacred paintings for churches and monasteries. Murillo's style progressed from an early hard, tight, line to a mature and flowing softness; his brilliant color is softened by a *sfumato* closer to that of Correggio than to Leonardo's; his madonnas and female saints have a gentle feminine charm, and they are draped in softly flowing robes and enveloped in even softer clouds. There is little traditional Spanish severity in Murillo and his own sincerity and sweetness of faith lend a pictorial quality to his works that make them encouraging and seductive; his religion is not frightening, but it is quite genuine and warm. Murillo did not confine himself to religious paintings and made portraits and composed *genre* scenes with equal grace and charm. His scenes of poor children portray them with sympathy and a humanitarianism that is quite modern in feeling. Murillo died after a fall from a scaffold while painting a large religious work for a convent in Cadiz, leaving behind a body of work that indicates that Spanish character has more than one aspect or that the grandeur of Velasquez had given way to a more dreamy rapture.

80

PIETER de HOOCH

Dutch

1629-c. 1688

AN INTERIOR

Reproduced by courtesy of the Trustees,
The National Gallery, London

Pieter de Hooch was born on the outskirts of Rotterdam, the son of a village butcher who fancied himself a painter. De Hooch was a pupil of Berchem in Haarlem until the age of twenty-three, when he became "painter and lackey" to a wealthy and eccentric merchant of Delft. In Delft, de Hooch felt the influence of Vermeer, an influence that shows in his using golden light as much as Vermeer used a silvery tone. Here too he met and married Jannetje van der Burch, daughter of a master faience maker. De Hooch was registered in the Delft Guild of Painters in 1655, but his name was stricken from the rolls, since he could not pay the dues. Jannetje died in 1667 and de Hooch, deeply affected by his young wife's death, moved to Amsterdam. His subjects, formerly charming portrayals of middle-class life and interiors, became scenes of upper-class life in Amsterdam. De Hooch's finest works are those he painted in Delft, for the straightforward simplicity of his style and his own temperament made the later fashionable scenes seem rather false. Note that a child is almost always portrayed. He died in Amsterdam at an unspecified date before 1688.

81

REMBRANDT HARMENSZOHN van RIJN
Dutch
1606-1669
NIGHT WATCH
Rijksmuseum, Amsterdam

Rembrandt Harmenszohn van Rijn, the greatest of all the Dutch painters and one of the greatest artists of all time, was born in Leyden, the son of a well-to-do miller who was ambitious enough to enroll his son in the Leyden Latin school. Young Rembrandt soon abandoned book learning to study painting, first in Leyden and then in Amsterdam, under Peter Lastman. After six months, Rembrandt, unlike other promising art students of his time, returned to Leyden rather than travel to Italy. He set up a studio and painted and sketched his parents, his sister, and the town burghers. In 1631 he moved permanently to Amsterdam. The first of his important commissions and great compositions, *The Anatomy Lesson of Dr. Tulp,* was painted in 1632. In 1634 he married Saskia van Uylenburch. She bore him four children of whom only Titus, the youngest, survived childhood. Saskia died in 1642. She had posed for many portraits, drawings, and etchings. For a time, Rembrandt's portraits found great favor, but as his work became greater and more spiritual, commissions dwindled and he suffered the tribulations of lawsuits and bankruptcy for debts acquired during his luxurious period of great success. His constant companion during these miserable years was Hendrickje Stoffels, a young servant who became

his lifelong companion and whom he could not marry because of a provision in Saskia's will that would have left Rembrandt and his beloved son penniless. Hendrickje, like Saskia, was a constant model. She gave him two daughters, the only children to survive Rembrandt. Hendrickje died about 1663, Titus in 1668, and Rembrandt in October, 1669. He painted constantly and his matchless art grew in splendor through many different and remarkable stages.

The Night Watch, with its complex composition of twenty-nine figures, was painted in 1642, during the middle period of Rembrandt's career. Preceded by the formative portraits of his youth and followed by the dark and mystical works of his last years, the middle period was that of his development of light, golden and rich, mystical and yet architectural in quality. Sitters of Rembrandt's time did not always appreciate the artist's skill, or his sensibility. Some of the members of Captain Banningh Cocq's company complained that their faces did not appear clearly enough in this golden glow and would have preferred a stronger light upon their faces. Protests were loud and foreshadowed the difficulties that Rembrandt's immortal genius would inflict upon him before his death.

82

CANALETTO

Italian

1697-1768

VENICE: THE QUAY OF THE PIAZZETTA

National Gallery of Art, Washington, D.C.
Gift of Mrs. Barbara Hutton

Giovanni Antonio Canal, known as Canaletto, was born in Venice where his father was a painter of theatrical scenery. The young Canaletto first studied in his father's workshop, then probably under the Dutch painter van Wittel. He next went to Rome, where he learned perspective from Panini, the famous architectural artist. Upon his return to Venice in 1720, Canaletto was immediately successful as a painter and engraver of city scenes. Among his early and enthusiastic patrons was Joseph Smith, the British consul, who urged him to go to Britain. Canaletto first went back to Rome

for a two year stay (1740-41) during which he painted Roman scenes, and made his first trip to England in 1745. Except for two trips to Venice he remained there until 1755. He painted many familiar English scenes and decorated many of the Palladian villas in the southern counties. He was elected to membership in the Venetian Academy in 1763. Canaletto had a large studio in Venice and turned out quantities of those paintings and etchings that have made his name synonymous with eighteenth-century Venice, the Pearl of the Adriatic, and Venetian life.

83

DIEGO RODRIGUEZ de SILVA y VELASQUEZ

Spanish

1599-1660

PORTRAIT DE L'INFANTE MARIE-MARGUERITE, FILLE DE PHILIPPE IV

Musée du Louvre, Paris

Diego Velasquez was born in Seville of Portuguese extraction. He may have studied with Herrara, but it is certain that he spent six years in Seville in the studio of a painter named Pacheco, whose daughter he married. His work, up until 1623, when he went to Madrid and became painter to the King, is quite Baroque in style, thick in pigment, sharp in contrast, and suitable for the tavern scenes and still life works he then painted. As court painter, he painted portraits principally and his manner changed entirely, becoming lighter and clearer, two-dimensional, and more Venetian and Flemish in general style. After a trip to Italy in 1629, Velasquez, who had copied Renaissance paintings and compared himself to the old masters, began to paint in fluid color and silvery tones, abandoned Classicism entirely, and painted in a manner that was not to be equalled, until the nineteenth-century Impressionists, for atmosphere, dramatic composition, use of light, and optical effects. Velasquez went again to Italy for the years 1649 to 1651 to collect old masters for the King. He managed to find time, however, to do a mag-

nificent portrait of Pope Innocent X. Upon his return to Madrid, Velasquez was made a Knight of the Order of Santiago and appointed Grand Marshall of the Palace. From then until his death, the artist had to devote much time to his royal duties and to cater to the royal whims. Velasquez died in 1660, as a result of the burden of his courtly duties.

Velasquez painted more portraits of this little princess, who was to become Empress of Austria at the age of fifteen, than of anybody else of the royal family. In *Portrait de l'Enfante Marguerite* she is about five or six years old, still soft and round with her baby flesh and pale gold hair. Against a harmonious background of shades of brown, the head of the child stands out like a flower or a patch of sunlight in a dark room. Her elaborate dress is painted in silvery tones of pearly grey, emphasized with black velvet. Combined with these are soft reds —ribbons, bows, and flowers, the latter dangling from a bracelet and clutched in a small hand. Something poignant comes out of this painting: such a little girl with such a weight upon her already.

84

JOHANNES VERMEER
Dutch
1632-1675
THE LETTER
Staatliche Kunstsammlungen Dresden, Gemäldegalerie Alte Meister

Johannes (Jan) Vermeer, known as "Vermeer of Delft," was born and died in that city, the son of a silk weaver and tavern owner who sold art as well as beer, not unusual for seventeenth-century Holland. Of Vermeer's life we know very little, for no documents have been preserved. He married Catherina Bolens in 1653 and was the father of eight children before his premature death at forty-three. He had inherited the tavern from his father and continued to run it as his father had, so that he was financially able to paint as he wished. It is certain that he attracted very little, if any, attention during his lifetime. In fact, it was not until 1860 that a monograph, written and published in Paris by Thoré (pseudonym, W. Bürger), an art critic, brought Vermeer to public notice and fame. Bürger listed sixty-six works as painted by Vermeer. About half of these are now accepted as authentic. Vermeer was a poet with the brush, creating a mystical timelessness in perfectly balanced, cool canvases in which predominant blues and pale golds are bathed in a silvery light.

A pale light from a hidden source suffuses *The Letter (Woman in Blue)*. The subject is framed as in the viewfinder of a camera. She stands reading forever, at the same time alone in a room in Delft and mysteriously someplace else, as we stand when we read a long-awaited letter— here . . . and there, with the writer . . . caught in an isolation so deep that nothing can disturb it. Vermeer saw this girl, but she did not see him. It is as simple as that.

85

ANTHONY van DYCK

Flemish

1599-1641

CHARLES I, KING OF ENGLAND

Musée du Louvre, Paris

Anthony van Dyck was born in Antwerp. He showed precocious talent, signed his first portrait in 1616, and was already well-known when he joined Rubens' workshop at about the age of twenty. He was Rubens' favorite pupil and most valued assistant, since he could imitate Rubens so well that it is almost impossible to distinguish the work of one from the other. Van Dyck went to England in 1620 upon the invitation of Charles I and spent a few months painting portraits. He then went to Italy for a short visit, back to Antwerp, and in either 1621 or 1622 returned to Italy for a stay of four years in Genoa. There he studied the works of the Italian masters and painted religious works. His work during this period shows the influence of Titian and the Venetian school. When he returned to Antwerp in 1627, he continued his painting of rather Baroque religious pictures and also completed a series of brilliant psychological portraits of contemporary poets and artists. He returned to England in 1632 as court painter to Charles I. During this period, which lasted until his early death, he painted 350 portraits, including 38 of the king and 35 of the queen. Van Dyck was extremely successful, very well-known, became very rich, and lived an extravagant life. His aristocratic and distinguished portraits were so much admired that they became the standard and the model for English portrait painting of the 17th century and an important historical record.

86

GEORGES de LA TOUR
French
1593-1652

ST. JOSEPH THE CARPENTER
Musée du Louvre, Paris

Georges de La Tour was born in Lorraine, in Vic-sur-Seille, of fairly humble origin. Knowledge of his work is a quite recent addition to the history of art, for even his name was lost until 1863 and no paintings were attached to his name until 1915, when Herman Voss identified a number of paintings that had previously been attributed to Caravaggio, Le Nain, Vermeer, and certain Spanish artists. By 1934, with the exhibition Peintres de la Réalité in Paris, it was clear that La Tour was a painter of considerable importance. Little more is known of his life than that he worked for the Duke of Lorraine during the plague and war years of 1631-1632, and rose to become painter to the King of France. His tenebrist or night style owes much to Caravaggio, but it seems probable that La Tour never went to Italy and derived this manner from the works of Honthorst, a contemporary Dutch painter who had lived in Italy for many years and had studied the works of the Italian masters. La Tour's night scenes dramatically lit

by shielded or unshielded candles and torches reveal in their primarily religious subjects a pure piety and a quiet, pensive mood. In his works, light surrounded by deep shadows falls on dense forms, distinctly outlined and in flat washes of color. His structure is as definite as that found in the works of Poussin and his religious feeling expressed by quiet, serious, and tender peasant faces in *genre* settings and poses is similar to that found in works by Le Nain. The deep concentration and focus of attention upon the central motifs of his paintings, a St. Sebastian, a child in the cradle, the puffing out of a candle flame, a flame itself, give them an ascetic, mystical, poetic importance, that increases as details become apparent, leaving an over-all impression of hushed silence, of human warmth in a vast wilderness. La Tour, who died in Lunéville, also in Lorraine, painted a few works lighted by the normal light of day: *genre* pictures, a St. Jerome with the same intense religious feeling, and a group of people intensely playing cards.

87

PETER PAUL RUBENS
Flemish
1577-1640
DANSE DE PAYSANS
Museo Nacional del Prado, Madrid

Peter Paul Rubens was born in Siegen. He became a member of the Antwerp Guild of St. Luke in 1598, and spent the years from 1600 to 1608 in Italy copying the works of the antique and older Italian masters and of his own contemporaries, Caravaggio, Cigoli, and the Carracci. In 1608, before returning to Antwerp, he visited Spain for the first time. He was to go again in 1628 and be dazzled by the work of Velasquez. 1609, the year of his first marriage, to Isabella Brandt, saw him made court painter to Archduke Albrecht and the Infanta Isabella. His first, or Italian, period produced such works as the series of the Twelve Apostles and the Alterpiece of Santa Trinità, Mantua. His second period, 1609 to 1614, covers the establishment of his studio and a change to his own style —unity in narrative action, bold lighting, and simplicity of figure. The third period, 1614 to 1622,

covers his mature style, much more fluid, with climactic movement, and great self-assurance. His fourth period, 1622 to 1632, was the time of his great commissions and is characterized by pictorialism. Rubens' first wife died in 1626 and in 1630 he married Helena Fourment, then aged seventeen. In the last years of his life his work was bathed in a golden glow, suffused with love and beauty, rich and warm in color. This account only briefly covers Rubens' life, for it is impossible to convey in so short a space the complexity of his activities. Rubens was the spirit of the seventeenth century, a gorgeous, sensuous, dramatic, powerful, and exuberant painter who turned life into a festival of beauty, infused it with new vitality, delighted in the antique and the pagan, and never lost his deep sense of religion nor his spiritual understanding and strong belief in his own faith.

88

FRANS HALS
Dutch
c. 1580-1666

LA BOHEMIENNE
Musée du Louvre, Paris

Frans Hals was born in Antwerp of Flemish parents. The Hals family moved to Haarlem when Hals was a boy and he spent the rest of his life there. He was a student of Karel van Mander from 1600 to 1603 before setting up his own workshop. It is a curious fact that although Hals received many public and private commissions, he seemed all his life to be short of money, and at the very end of his life became the recipient of a pension of 200 guilders a year voted by the Haarlem Town Council. Hals is best known for his portraits of tavern entertainers, soldiers, and other picturesque characters, for his great group portraits remain in Haarlem in the buildings for which they were commissioned. In them we may trace his artistic progress. Early work shows loose composition, bright, showy color, and little regard for individual likeness. His works later became tightly composed, more subdued in color, and psychologically penetrating. His last two great works for the old men's hospital are painted in variations of a subtle dark gray and the characterization is dignified and strong. Hals' noncommissioned portraits are notable for their bursting vitality, lightning brushwork, and brilliant lighting and color. For the last two years of his life, Hals, then a town pensionee, did not paint at all.

La Bohemienne literally bursts with life and exuberant youthful high spirits. Color glows in bright red, white, and pale blue-green, against which a cloud of hair seems almost to move in this arrested moment. Light comes from above and the left, a characteristic touch of Hals, and passes across and down. A secondary source of light starts at the right, and the focus of the two beams is the apple-cheeked, smiling face. It is hard to believe that Hals spent most of his life worrying about money, while portraying such happy people with such gusto, as if they had not a care in the world.

89

EL GRECO

Spanish

c. 1541-1614

VIEW OF TOLEDO

The Metropolitan Museum of Art, New York
Bequest of Mrs. H. O. Havemeyer, 1929
The H. O. Havemeyer Collection

Domenico Theotocopuli, called El Greco, was born in Crete, where he received his first training in the Byzantine style. Theotocopuli is presumed to have left Crete in about 1560 for Venice, where he probably studied with Titian and had considerable contact with Tintoretto. He then went to Rome, where he studied the work of Michelangelo and Raphael. In 1577 he went to Toledo, the former capital of Spain and a center for Greeks who opposed Turkish rule. The Spaniards discarded his Greek name and simply called him "El Greco." Spain was then in the grip of the Inquisition under the despotic and fanatical rule of Philip the Second. Philip, it is said, loved painting almost as much as he did religion, and he commissioned El Greco to do a work for the Escorial. The work, *The Legend of St. Maurice,* a masterpiece of spiritual and humanistic art, did not please the King. El Greco's next great work was his view of Toledo,

bathed in a Surrealistic light, its craggy ramparts standing out against an ethereal sky as they rise from the arid landscape. As one approaches Toledo today from Madrid, one sees the painter's vision of the city; it has not changed. El Greco, the most moving and the most mystical of all the religious painters, created for Spain, from his Greek and Italian training, the first truly national Spanish art. He lived in Toledo, at first wealthy and then very poor, until his death, leaving to the city and to Spain a fabulous treasury of art.

El Greco's paintings reflect the intense and morbid religious feeling of Spain under the Inquisition. The King may not have appreciated the artist's work, but the Church commissioned him very often. We find in El Greco today both a haunting memory of the sixteenth century and a feeling of awe at his own intensely spiritual visions.

90

PIETER BRUEGHEL, the ELDER
Flemish
c. 1525/30-1569
WINTER LANDSCAPE
Delporte Collection

Pieter Brueghel was born in either the Flemish town of Brueghel or Breda. According to the Dutch historian van Mander, he studied in Antwerp, first with Pieter Coecke van Aelst and then, in about 1550, with Hieronymous Cock. He was a registered and active member of the Antwerp Guild in 1551, the year in which he embarked on a long trip to Italy, going as far as Sicily and making sketches from nature on his voyage. Upon his return to Antwerp, in or shortly before 1555, he made drawings for etchings done by Hieronymous Cock. He finally settled in Brussels in about 1563 and married a daughter of Pieter Coecke, with whom he had two sons. Brueghel lived peacefully in Brussels and had a successful life as a painter and a stimulating one as a member of a Humanist group of distinguished liberals. Brueghel's paintings, all of which have a moral and humanistic significance, date from the years 1556-1568. He painted *genre* pictures of peasant life indicative of his belief that the peasant, although rough, was not vulgar, for he was a natural man; fantastic scenes on literary bases, using proverbs as a starting point; and religious subjects, treated as great cosmic landscapes peopled with peasants. His primary concern was for mankind and his principal belief was in the power of nature and of life. Brueghel died in 1569, leaving his sons to continue painting in the manner he had begun.

The simplicity of the statement in *Winter Landscape* makes this work delightful; the pale, simple colors, white, yellows, blacks, pale grays, make it beautiful; and the movement of the little figures make it a joy to examine.

91

VERONESE
Italian
1528-1588

THE WEDDING AT CANA

Musée du Louvre, Paris

Veronese (Paolo Caliari) was born in Verona, where he first studied sculpture with his father, Gabriele Caliari, before taking up the study of painting with Antonio Badile. Veronese travelled to Castelfranco, Vicenza, and Siena. In 1552 he painted an altarpiece for the cathedral in Mantua, decorations for the Villa Emo in Fanzole, and other works, before going to Venice in 1555 to settle down for the rest of his life. Veronese received many commissions for decorative work in villas in the vicinity of Venice and was called in to decorate the Doges' Palace after the great fires of 1574 and 1577. He produced large altarpieces and many elaborately rich mythological and allegorical subjects—famous banquet and wedding scenes with Biblical subjects treated contemporaneously. He was the painter *par excellence* of Venetian pomp and splendor, painting in cool, clear color, and arranging hundreds of richly dressed figures completely at ease in superb renditions of silk and velvet, and jewels. Veronese, in fact, set the standard for Venetian decoration of the 18th century.

92

TINTORETTO

Italian

1518-1594

ALLEGORY OF FIDELITY

Courtesy of the Fogg Art Museum, Harvard University
Gift of Mrs. Samuel Sachs, in Memory of Mr. Samuel Sachs

Jacopo Robusti called Tintoretto, the "little dyer," because his father was a dyer by trade, was born in Venice. Tintoretto, who studied for a short time with Titian, and then with Schiavone, admired the color of Titian and the drawing of Michelangelo. He stated clearly that he intended to combine color and drawing to create a new form of art. His painting, intensely personal, inventive in the highest degree, dramatic, appealing to the imagination, was to become increasingly Mannerist in style as it grew more and more fluid through the years. He painted portraits, classical or mythological works, and religious canvases using Old Testament themes and subjects. His portraits are restrained and intimate, tightly painted, glowing with color, and extremely effective. His classical works are distinguished by their flowing grace and the injection of dramatic elements into poetic conceptions. Tintoretto's inventive genius shows best, however, in the many paintings he created to decorate the Palace of the Doges, various Venetian churches, the Scuolo della Trinità, and the Scuolo di San Rocco. In these enormous compositions, some of them 30 feet long, he created mysterious scenes full of unearthly light, realistic historical landscapes, or elaborate court interiors—all of them crowded with figures in extraordinary positions, carefully dressed in crackingly textured fabrics, and with pearly flesh upon which light coming from diversified and multiple sources plays with as much rapidity as the works were painted. In his great canvases on the life of Christ for the Scuolo di San Rocco, Tintoretto's personal vision reached its culmination. In an explosive and passionate expression of the inherent drama of the story, foreshortened perspective, dramatic points of view, light pouring from every angle—as much a part of the paintings as the subjects—and human figures exalted, tormented, or struggling with the forces of nature and the spirit, Tintoretto reveals himself as realist and dreamer, as tragic and poetic. This complete separation from traditional concepts not only influenced Mannerists, but found further distillation in the works of El Greco.

93

CORREGGIO
Italian
1489/1494-1534
ANTIOPE SLEEPING
Musée du Louvre, Paris

Antonio Allegri, the most important of the Baroque painters of the High Renaissance was born in Correggio, hence the name by which he is known. The nephew of Lorenzo Allegri, a painter with whom he may have studied, he became a pupil of Antonio Bartolloti in his native city. Correggio is known to have visited Mantua and Parma where he saw the works of Venetian artists, and, although he probably never went to Rome, he had seen works of Mantegna, Leonardo da Vinci, Michelangelo, and Raphael, but was not influenced by the classical balance of the latter two painters' works. Correggio's own work is bold in perspective, free in movement, and emotionally voluptuous, full of a joy in physical existence that often reaches the ecstatic, and endowed with softness of texture and exquisite color. In 1514, Correggio returned to his own town and worked in the Palazzo dei Signorie and painted an altarpiece for a church. His first fresco was painted in Parma, in 1518, for the private quarters of the Abbess of the Convent of San Paolo. The work was an allegorical rendering of the myth of Diana. Correggio returned home in the following year to marry and then went back to Parma to remain for ten years,

until the death of his wife. It was in Parma that he painted his largest and greatest work in the dome of the Cathedral. Here, his perspective opens out into a dream heaven of tumbling and dancing figures for whom gravity does not exist in spite of their very real physical bodies. The result is a painting, *The Assumption of the Virgin,* that is both a spiritual and physical pleasure and a true masterpiece. In addition to his many altarpieces and frescoes, Correggio painted, for the Duke of Mantua and Isabella d'Este, a series of erotic mythological works: *Jupiter and Io,* the *Danaë, Leda, Antiope, Ganymede.* Graceful, elegant, and delicately sensuous, these works combine, as do his sacred paintings, the airy *sfumato* of Leonardo, Michelangelo's architectural *disegno,* and his own particularly beautiful landscape backgrounds, luscious painting of flesh, soft color, delicate texture, abandonment of pose, and energetic life. Correggio died quite young, according to Vasari of a fever following a long walk in the hot sun and a drink of water. His influence in the years immediately after his death was slight, but by 1600 he began to be recognized for his individual worth and as the peer of Raphael and Michelangelo.

94

HANS HOLBEIN, the YOUNGER

German

1497/98-1543

ANNE OF CLEVES

Musée du Louvre, Paris

Hans Holbein, the Younger, was born in Augsburg. His father, a fine painter in his own right, gave young Hans his first lessons in art. Holbein went to live in Basel, Switzerland, as a young man of about seventeen, and came in contact with the Humanists of the flourishing city. He acquired Swiss citizenship in 1526, but before that date had become a member of the Basel guild of artists and received many commissions for paintings and designs for glass and woodcuts. In 1515 Holbein illustrated *The Praise of Folly* by Erasmus, though he did not meet the Dutch philosopher until some years later. It was through Erasmus that Holbein went to England in 1526 to remain for two years working for Henry the Eighth and beginning a portrait of the family of Sir Thomas More. Holbein returned to Basel and worked there until 1532, when he went back to England to stay for the rest of his life. He worked in England for the King and for the court, as well as for many ambassadors and foreign residents. Holbein's portraits are vivid likenesses with much detail and they create a gallery that remains one of the most important pictorial histories depicting a most fascinating era.

95

TITIAN
Italian
c. 1477-1576

L'HOMME AU GANT
Musée du Louvre, Paris

Titian was born Tiziano Vecelli in Pieve di Cadore, north of Venice. He came to Venice early as an apprentice to Sebastiano Zuccato, before studying with the Bellinis. In about 1508 he worked with Giorgione on the frescoes of the Fondaco dei Tedeschi, and in 1510 he left Venice to escape the outbreak of the plague that killed Giorgione. In 1512 he returned from Padua, where he had painted frescoes of *The Life of St. Anthony,* and in 1516 became the official painter of the Venetian Republic, but also worked for the Duke d'Este in Ferrara and the Duke di Gonzaga in Mantua. During the next fifteen years Titian painted altarpieces, private devotional paintings, mythological subjects, and formal portraits. In 1548 Emperor Charles V called Titian to Augsburg, where he painted many portraits. When the artist returned to Venice, he was rich, famous, and highly honored. He bought a large house and entertained the society of Europe. His paintings of the people who visited him are rich historical documents as well as magnificent works of art. He continued to paint until his death in 1576. Titian is the greatest painter of the Venetian Renaissance and one of the greatest painters who ever lived. His work is magnificent in color, in tonal quality, in movement, in composition, in comprehension of drama and greatness, in psychological insight, and in, more simply, painting. His influence upon the great painters who followed him in time has been enormous. Titian's art passed in style from the High Renaissance, through Mannerism to the Baroque. In all of these styles he was magical in color and titanic in concept, the epitome of the excellencies of painting and the sum of the genius of Venetian Renaissance art in all its full glory.

96

MICHELANGELO BUONARROTI
Italian
1475-1564
DELPHIC SYBIL
Sistine Chapel, Vatican, Rome

Michelagniolo di Lodovico di Lionardo di Buonarroti Simone was born in Caprese in Tuscany. The son of a civil servant, he attended Latin School and then studied painting in the workshop of the Ghirlandaio brothers and sculpture with Bertoldo, a former pupil of Donatello. Michelangelo's early training derived from the great Florentine masters of the Low Renaissance: Giotto, Masaccio, Donatello, and Signorelli. A typical Renaissance man, he was gifted as a painter, a sculptor, an architect, an engineer, and a poet, but his preference was for sculpture with its plastic possibilities for the revelation and exaltation of the human body. By the time he was fifteen, he had attracted the attention of Lorenzo de' Medici and was invited to join the scholars, writers, and artists who frequented the Medici palace. This early experience and exposure to Neo-Platonic thought influenced his ideals and concepts throughout his life. Michelangelo began as a sculptor and made his first statues between 1496 and 1501 in Rome. His first and only certain easel painting was painted in about 1503, a *tondo* of *The Holy Family* in a closely-knit triangular composition that might have been cut from a single block of stone. Michelangelo's life coincided with a period of enormous papal power and from 1505 when he signed the contract for the Tomb of Pope Julius, he was subject to political pressures, wars, and papal orders and counter-orders. His greatest painting, the decoration of the Sistine Chapel was painted single-handed, between 1508 and 1512, when the project for the tomb was dropped. The awe-inspiring, monumental work represents scenes of the Creation and the Old Testament through the story of Noah, and begins with Adam receiving the spark of divine life from God. The symbolic themes, divided architectonically, present a complicated vision, miraculous in its variety and complete unification. Above the niches in which sit the prophets and the sybils, the *ignudi,* nude athletes, flank the central scenes where definite historical settings alternate with extra-spatial and extra-temporal visions, glorifying the human body and the spirit of mankind. In 1537, Michelangelo began his *Last Judgment,* the fresco on the far wall of the chapel. Here sculptural and architectural vision is replaced by swirling space and more pictorial representation of tortured humans corresponding to the artist's own unhappiness, frustrations, and increasing religious doubts. In this and in his last paintings, (1541-1550) for the Paolino Chapel, Michelangelo was no longer the exponent of Classicism, but the forerunner of the Mannerist School. Thus, this lonely, unhappy genius influenced first Raphael, whose work sums up the best of the Classical Renaissance, and then Correggio, Tintoretto, and countless other painters who have succeeded him through the centuries, while his own super-human concepts still fascinate and torment the world's scholars; concepts that will hold their fascination for all time.

DELPHICA

97

ALBRECHT DURER

German

1471-1528

PRAYING HANDS

Graphische Sammlung Albertina, Vienna

Albrecht Dürer was born in Nürnberg. His father was a goldsmith from Hungary, and it was in his father's shop that Dürer learned the techniques he later applied to his woodcuts and etchings. Dürer's early talent convinced his father that the boy must have training in art. He was first apprenticed to a painter and then sent to travel throughout Europe. He remained away for four years, visiting Colmar, Basel, Strasburg, and Venice. He then returned to Nürnberg for ten years, painting and engraving. Upon his second trip to Italy, in 1505, Dürer found himself greeted with respect and admiration, for his fame had spread from the printing press he had set up in Nürnberg for the reproduction of his own works. An original and lively artist, Dürer is best known for his graphics, which have been better preserved than his paintings, many of which have been seriously damaged. His importance in the world of art rests upon his Humanistic point of view, his great talent, and his intellectual perception. Dürer died young—he was only fifty-seven—but he left behind a body of work that includes many masterpieces of the field of engraving.

Praying Hands is familiar to us in plaster casts, in wood, and in marble. It is in the original drawing that we may see most clearly the fine detail. The hands are not only beautiful but entirely expressive of honest religious belief and gentle piety. Old, heavily veined, naturally graceful, they seem familiar, safe hands to trust, capable and warm.